MASON JAR
NATION

THE JARS THAT CHANGED AMERICA
AND
ᔆ 50 ᔆ
CLEVER WAYS TO USE THEM TODAY

JOANN MOSER

COOL
SPRINGS
PRESS
Home and Garden Experts™

MINNEAPOLIS, MINNESOTA

Quarto is the authority on a wide range of topics.

Quarto educates, entertains and enriches the lives of our readers—enthusiasts and lovers of hands-on living.

www.quartoknows.com

© 2016 Quarto Publishing Group USA Inc.

Photography © JoAnn Moser;
pages 19, 20, 21, 22, 23 (top photo), 24, 26 © Library of Congress.

First published in 2016 by Cool Springs Press, an imprint of
Quarto Publishing Group USA Inc., 400 First Avenue North, Suite 400,
Minneapolis, MN 55401 USA.
Telephone: (612) 344-8100 Fax: (612) 344-8692

quartoknows.com
Visit our blogs at quartoknows.com

Cool Springs Press titles are also available at discounts in bulk quantity for industrial or sales-promotional use. For details contact the Special Sales Manager at
Quarto Publishing Group USA Inc.,
400 First Avenue North, Suite 400, Minneapolis, MN 55401 USA.

10 9 8 7 6 5 4 3 2 1

ISBN: 978-1-59186-652-7

Library of Congress Cataloging-in-Publication Data

Names: Moser, JoAnn, 1963- author.
Title: Mason jar nation : the jars that changed America and
50 clever ways to use them today / JoAnn Moser.
Description: Minneapolis, MN, USA : Cool Springs Press, 2016.
Identifiers: LCCN 2015047475 | ISBN 9781591866527 (paperback)
Subjects: LCSH: Glass craft. | Handicraft--Materials. | Storage jars. |
BISAC: CRAFTS & HOBBIES / Glass & Glassware.
Classification: LCC TT298 .M67 2016 | DDC 748.5028--dc23
LC record available at http://lccn.loc.gov/2015047475

Acquiring Editor: Mark Johanson
Project Manager: Alyssa Bluhm
Art Director: Brad Springer
Cover Design: Faceout Studio
Interior Design: Rob Johnson
Layout: Brad Norr

Printed in China

DEDICATION

For Nick, who has the tools and the talent.

....

ACKNOWLEDGMENTS

First, I'd like to thank all the fabulous people at Cool
Springs Press who made this book possible. Specifically
Mark Johanson, for trusting me to bring his idea to
fruition; Brad Springer, for making everything look better;
and Alyssa Bluhm, for helping me cross the finish line.

Much appreciation goes to John and Becky Varone.
John's vast knowledge of vintage fruit jars and their closures
is rivaled only by his magnificent fruit jar collection.
His willingness to share both put me on a solid path.

Special thanks to the very photogenic Gavin, Garrett,
and Abby. And to Nick, who never flinches when I say,
"I have an idea."

Contents

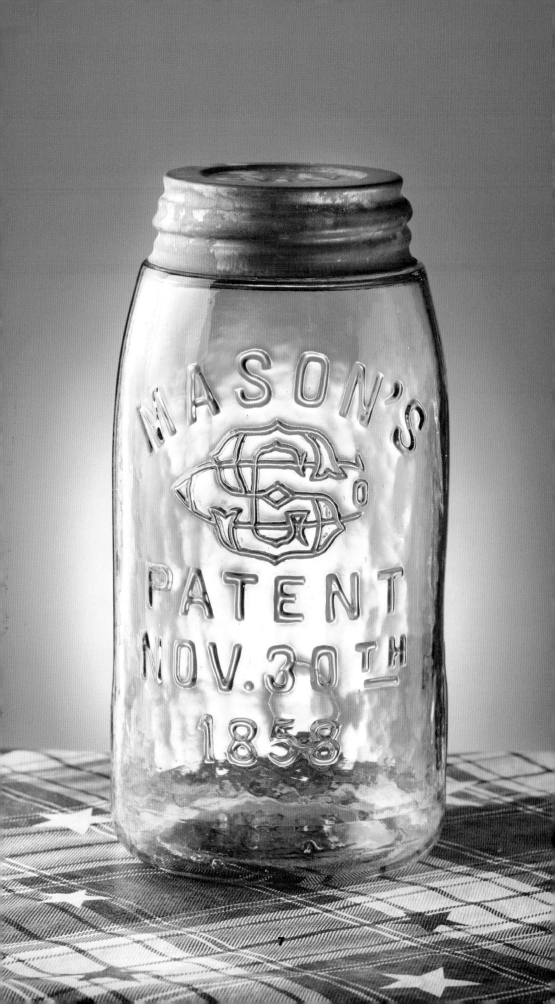

Introduction

I'm a writer who likes to make stuff. I've been doing both all my life. So when approached to write a book about clever ways to use Mason jars, I jumped at the opportunity. When my editor also suggested that the book include history and collectible information about Mason jars, I came down with a case of the nerves. Then I remembered how much I like research. I happily let myself spend hour upon hour tracking down out-of-print books, following links into ever-widening Internet circles, and sending emails to perfect strangers who know more about the subject than I do.

One such email exchange ended with an invitation to a local antique glass and bottle show. While there, I

A fraction of John's jar collection shown with an assortment of vintage jar wrenches.

told one of the show's organizers about my project. "Mason jars?" he said. "You want to talk to that guy right over there." He pointed to a sprightly man of retirement age standing at a table on which were displayed a handful of jars. "He has one of the best fruit jar collections in the state, if not in the country." I thanked him kindly and made a beeline to "that guy."

Another introduction was made. "My name's John," he said, and about 30 seconds after that I realized I had struck gold. This wasn't just "that" guy; this was *the* guy. I spoke to John for a half an hour or so, but it didn't take long for him to invite me to his home to meet his wife and to see his collection.

"Could I take pictures of some of your jars for my book?" I asked.

"Sure!" he said.

About a week later, I was at John's house, not exactly believing what I was seeing. "This is an original Mason Jar? Like a John *Mason* Mason jar?"

He nodded and then told me the story of how he acquired it. (Through eBay, if you're wondering.)

I never knew it was possible to be star-struck by an inanimate object, but I was then.

John went on to show me an amber quart-size Kerr jar that "Alex" gave to him.

"Alex?" I asked.

"Alex Kerr," he said. "Grandson of the original."

(Of course, *Alex*!)

"And this one?" I pointed to a particularly charming jar, on it an image of a beaver munching away on a log.

"Canadian," he said. "The one you really want is the one with the beaver facing left. Now *that* one is very rare."

(Beaver facing left. Got it.)

During our afternoon together, John dropped names like Atlas, Cohansey, and Hero. One after another, he described unique jar closures, a topic about which John is particularly passionate. He pointed to this jar and that, each with a story behind it—where it was made, who made it, how it was made, and, of course, how he came to acquire it.

I realized these weren't just fruit jars we were talking about. They were slices of history, both America's and one man's.

When I left John's house that day, I was determined to hit my musty old books, follow those links even if they took me down rabbit holes, and submerge myself in Mason jar history.

And that's where this book starts: in the past. We'll look at some of the heavy hitters of the fruit jar game, including why the terms "Mason jar" and "fruit jar" have become synonymous. We'll see how the simple containers impacted US history and how history impacted the jars themselves.

Then we'll cover some jar-collecting basics, including tips to help you identify a fruit jar's age, where to buy jars and what prices to expect, and how to collect so you don't become overwhelmed.

We'll also further explore the history of Mason jars. I'll offer up the names of some of my favorite websites pertaining to the topic as well as several invaluable books I've accumulated doing research.

Before we get to the projects, we'll take a quick-but-necessary detour discussing techniques—including safety precautions—used when working with jars as craft items.

As for the projects that made the cut, they had to be fun to make, but also useful—like the jars themselves. Whether they hold a tasty treat or they add a bit of beauty to your world, I hope the projects featured in this book will be just that.

History

As with many things in American history, the Mason jar's story begins in Europe—specifically France—with a gentleman named Nicolas Appert. Born in 1750, Appert grew up to be a maestro in the culinary world. Not only was he a chef; he was also a baker, a pickler, a preserver, and a brewmaster. It's no surprise then that, in 1795, it was Appert who accepted Napoleon's challenge to devise a means of preserving food for military consumption. It was the emperor who said, "An army marches on its stomach," and those stomachs have to be well nourished, especially if you have dreams of world domination. Ultimately, it would take the next 14 years for Appert to perfect what became known as "Appertizing"—or what we now call "canning"—and win the emperor's prize of 12,000 francs for doing so.

Not only was Appert the grandfather of today's preserving techniques, but he was also the inventor

---

Fruit jars, circa 1850s to 1860s. The flanged lip of the jar on the left—the oldest of the group—was constructed as a means to tie string or rawhide to keep the closure intact, which itself may have been rawhide or even paper. The center jar's closure incorporated a flat disk that fit inside the channel; hot wax was poured into the reservoir to complete the seal. The jar on the right would have been closed with a simple stopper.

of the first modern-day fruit jar. In his seminal work describing his processes, *L'art de conserver les substances animales et vegetables*, Appert tells us that he used glass bottles made for his "special use." The bottles had necks that were 2 to 4 inches in diameter, and they were "of equal thickness in every part to prevent breaking." The one thing his bottles lacked was threads. For closures, Appert used corks, which he tapped into place with a whack of a "bat," then secured them with wire and finished their seals by applying a homemade luting.

Appert's attention to corks cannot be overstated, as he predicated the success of Appertizing on closures first and boiling the jars and their contents second. Home canners successfully used Appert's technique for 50 years before Louis Pasteur explained that it was the boiling process during canning that killed the microbes that caused food to spoil.

At this point, the fruit jar's advancement takes a detour into tinsmithing, when on August 30, 1810, merchant Peter Durand filed a British patent describing a process of using a variety of containers in which to preserve food, including "vessels of glass, pottery, tin or other metals or fit materials." (Later, Durand would file another patent for the tinned can itself.) It is from Durand's description that future patent applications referred to glass containers as glass canisters or "glass cans," for the sake of brevity. This is most likely why we call the preserving process "canning" and not "jarring," etymologically speaking.

The next big thing to happen to glass jars via tin smithery was Robert Arthur's 1855 patent for a self-sealing tin can. In it, he described a technique of manufacture that utilized a channel at the mouth of a can, which could be filled with an adhesive cement into which a cover would be set, creating a hermetic seal.

Considering that previous can-sealing methods required soldering, this might have been a breakthrough for the home-canning industry, but it wasn't. Not everyone was a fan. Cans were expensive, they weren't reusable, consumers couldn't see the contents inside them, and the acidity of the food reacted to the metal in an unappetizing way. These were just a few reasons why canning was still primarily a commercial endeavor at the time.

Those who benefited the most from the advancement in the food-canning trade were large institutions, such as hospitals and, as Napoleon had hoped, the military. Cans travelled well, and no longer did soldiers and sailors have to rely on dried meat, smoked fish, and fermented cabbage to satiate their hunger. They could use a chisel to pop off the top of a can and dive in. The downside of not being able to see the cans' contents remained, which meant consumers might not know until the containers were opened if the food inside was fit to eat. That could be a problem if you were on a ship in the middle of the sea or crossing great divides searching for a new settlement.

Although glass blowers had been making their own advancements from Appert's cork-sealing days, they were still left with only two ways to finish a jar's lip: pressing it or grinding it. The first method was fine for making a press-on, self-sealing lid, but it didn't allow for creation of screw threads. The second method didn't allow for sealing at the lip because the grind left a rough, potentially leaky surface.

The birth of the Mason jar

But a game change was on the horizon. On November 30, 1858, at the age of 26, John L. Mason, former farm boy from New Jersey, filed a patent with the US Patent Office and made history with a newfangled type of fruit jar closure.

A tinsmith by trade, Mason devised a revolutionary closing method for creating a jar with threads that vanished below a jar's lip and before its shoulder, thus creating a hermetic seal. As Mason's expertise was not in glassmaking, he licensed others to make his jars—most notably the shop owned by Samuel Crowley whose glass blower, Clayton Parker, made the first Mason jars.

Subsequently, Mason licensed others to make his jars' caps as well. His choices for licensing the production out to separate entities set the precedent for jars and their caps to be sold separately for the next 20 years, which is why Mason jars, for the most part, have interchangeable lids. An Atlas lid fits on a Ball jar, a Ball lid fits on a Presto jar, and so on.

One might wonder how a young tinsmith—with no glass-blowing experience, mind you—was able to conjure up a brilliant idea like vanishing threads. In his work, *Fruit*

Parts of a Mason jar. The addition of the bead first appeared in the early 1900s. It was originally incorporated into the design as a means to make the jar's neck stronger. Only later was it used as a sealing surface.

An original shoulder seal Mason jar embossed with the inventor's November 30, 1858, patent date.

jar's shoulder. The problem with this type of closure was that the shoulders oftentimes didn't withstand the force of twisting on the one-piece lid and broke, making the food that had been inside dangerous to consume.

In addition to the jars' weak shoulders, Mason's lids, which were made of zinc, literally left a bad taste in people's mouths—as they imparted a metallic flavor to the jars' contents. This alone spurred glassmakers and tinsmiths alike, including Mason himself, to devise and file hundreds and hundreds of jar closure patents, trying to best

Jars, Julian Harrison Toulouse recounts a story of Mason visiting famed mold maker William Brooke two to three years before Mason filed his patent. Mason and another gentleman visited Brooke's shop, where, according to Brooke's son, they inquired about the possibility of making a mold for a watertight jar. Brooke Sr. in turn described a concept that would do the job: the vanishing-thread technique.

Whether this exchange happened or not, Mason was the one who had the foresight to run with the idea. And run he did.

The search for closure
Although the world now had a more reliable way of closing fruit jars than Appert's cork and bat route, Mason's patent wasn't without its flaws. Because the jars needed to have threads, their lips had to be ground, which meant they couldn't seal on the lip. (Remember, grinding equals leaks.) That left one *other* place for the seal: the

Rare Eagle jar, circa 1860 to 1865, with a glass lid and spring-steel band clip.

A collection of Boyd's glass-lined lids. Interestingly, fruit jar lids and jars were sold separately until about 1890.

in towns with a corner grocery store. Closures aside, the process of home canning was grueling back then as the equipment used wasn't exactly state-of-the-art. After all that work, even the most meticulous of canners could end up with less than stellar outcomes. Metallic-tasting string beans. Moldy peaches. Broken bits of glass in strawberry preserves. The last of these was caused by those weak shoulders mentioned earlier or the overzealous use of a hammer and screwdriver to remove a stuck lid.

It's not surprising that enthusiasm for home canning in the United States didn't really start to catch on until after the Civil War when, in the spring of 1869, Lewis Boyd rescued the nation's collective taste buds by devising an opal glass plate that could line Mason's zinc lids. By this time Boyd was the holder of five of Mason's original patents—including that for the Mason jar—as he'd bought them in 1859.

Possibly to buff a bit of tarnish off his name, Mason started developing a top-sealing series of jars in the same year Boyd came out with the Boyd glass liners. But this last desperate push couldn't save what was left of Mason's fortune, for in 1870 the original patent for the Mason jar expired. Hundreds and hundreds of glass manufacturers swooped in, picked up the patent date *and* his name, and unabashedly printed them on their jars. That's when the name Mason became ubiquitous, and why Mason is now the Kleenex of kleenexes and the Hoover of hoovering. It's also why the jar featured on the cover of this book is embossed with the Swayzee Glass Company (S.G.Co.) logo as well as the Mason name and patent date.

Mason's original design, or rather, overcome its flaws.

Clips, cam levers, wire bails, yokes and thumb wheels—you name it; someone invented it as a means to find a better sealing method. Often paired with glass lids, these closures weren't the most practical, as glass didn't perform very well under pressure. Since these glass lids broke so easily, they (and their jars), with their complicated closures, are some of the rarest on the collectible fruit jar market today.

Why all the competition in the race to find a perfect, easy-to-use closure? Because food storage meant survival. Not everyone lived

The Mason jar goes mainstream

If William Brooke were still with us today, he might say the appropriation of Mason's name by other glassmakers of the day was payback for Mason's past transgressions, but in the fruit jar collecting world, it is nothing more than the blatant theft of the only thing Mason had left of value. After a life of early successes and a fruitful marriage that produced eight daughters, Mason died penniless in 1902 at the age of 70. He was a charity patient at New York City's House of Relief.

If the fruit jar-making business were a relay race, this is the stretch where Frank and Edmund Ball would pick up the baton. The brothers' introduction to the glassmaking business began in 1880 in Buffalo, New York, making wood-jacketed metal cans used to hold kerosene. After a fire destroyed their facility, they moved to another where they were joined by their three brothers, William, Lucius, and George. Soon they added a wood-jacketed glass jug to their product line and dove headfirst into the glassmaking business. It was then they started to produce fruit jars, whose patent was now in the public domain, and emblazoned them with the Ball Brothers Glass Manufacturing Company emblem, BBGM CO (see page 27). Referred to as "Buffalo Jars," they are among the rarest in fruit jar collecting, as they were only manufactured from 1885 to 1886. That's because, once again, the Ball factory went up in flames.

Enticed by abundant natural gas reserves, the city officials' gift of seven acres of land, $5,000, and a rail line to their future factory, the Ball brothers moved their operations from Buffalo, New York, to Muncie, Indiana. By 1888, things were up and running.

The Ball brothers' contribution to Muncie's growth as a city parallels their threefold contribution to the fruit jar industry, which included salesmanship, mechanization, and research of canning processes.

Not only did Ball sell their own jars, but they sold other smaller job shops' inventory as well—serving as a dealer of sorts. Between the selling fees, which the other shops had to pay the brothers, and the company's large sales force, their competitors didn't stand a chance.

In their quest for automation, the brothers developed the Ball-Bingham, a powered glass-blowing machine. With its inception, jar production increased dramatically, thereby flooding the market with the Ball brand. As the nineteenth century neared its end, Ball was producing 25 percent of the nation's fruit jars, manufacturing just shy of 13 million jars a year. At that time, they employed more than a thousand workers and had expanded their operations to include zinc lids, metal stamping, and rubber gaskets. To maintain control over every aspect of their enterprise, the brothers bought zinc mills to make lids, and strawboard factories to make their own shipping crates. During this expansion, jar production continued to flourish. At the turn of the century, they were producing 40 million jars a year, and in 1905, that number jumped to a whopping 74 million.

As for its influence on research, Ball partnered with colleges, establishing fellowships that focused on agricultural home economics studies. The brothers brought their knowledge into the household in 1909 when they published their first *Blue Book*, a pamphlet that included canning instructions and recipes.

The marriage of lid and jar

While the Ball brothers were taking over the jar market, grocery wholesaler Alexander H. Kerr was breaking into the lid game. In 1915, he filed a patent with the US Patent Office for a jar lid with an integrated sealing compound that would flow when heated, creating a hermetic top seal on any jars that had a smooth, machine-made lip. The lid was held in place by a threaded band. The precursor of what is still used today, the two-piece sealing method eventually caught on as glassmaking machines became more sophisticated and, therefore, reliable in making the smooth jar tops necessary for the lids to function properly.

Up until the early part of the twentieth century, jars were produced with what is now considered a standard, regular-mouth opening of approximately 2½". It was Kerr who, in 1920, started producing jars with a 3" opening, which he dubbed "wide-mouth." Soon thereafter, Ball copied the design and started producing wide-mouth jars as well.

When Alexander Kerr died in 1925, his son Thomas oversaw operations of The Kerr Glass Manufacturing Company, then located in Sand Springs, Oklahoma, until his own death five years later. Rose Kerr, Alexander's third wife, took the reins in 1930 and her place as the first woman executive in the glass-blowing industry—if not one of the first women executives in manufacturing—in the United States.

A rare, circa 1899, Ball jar with bail and wire "lightning" closure, so called for its ease of opening. The lightning closure patent for fruit jars is attributed to Henry W. Putnam (1882), its impetus a design by Charles de Quillfeldt that was used for closing bottles.

Mason jar nation

As Rose Kerr attended to the jar-making business, women of more modest means were running their own production lines, of sorts, out of their kitchens. Thanks to canning, no longer did they or their families exist on feast-or-famine diets. They could eat "fresh" fruit and vegetables that they had grown during times of feast throughout the famine times of winter. Their endeavors were promulgated by the government in 1910, with the USDA's first-ever publication, titled *Canning Vegetables in the Home*. The pamphlet included everything a home canner might need to know about canning techniques of the day, including the science behind the process, kinds of containers to use (glass being the most satisfactory), selecting the right fruits and vegetables, and even how to open jars. The booklet assured the reader that, "If you follow the directions here given carefully, you will have no difficulty whatever."

With the advent of World War I, people were encouraged, and taught via local food boards, to can fresh fruits and vegetables that couldn't easily be transported overseas. Because of the population's self-rationing and commitment to reduce waste, food consumption in the United States dropped 15 percent between 1918 and 1919. The reduction allowed the country to redirect the 18,500,000 tons of food surplus it created to troops

Woman with a collection of preserved goods, including peas, beans, fruit, and eggs, circa 1917 to 1919.

and Allies overseas during the same period. After the war, President Herbert Hoover continued to organize food shipments to famine-plagued areas of central Europe.

As things heated up overseas, a quiet revolution of sorts was happening in the southern United States—namely, Tomato Clubs. Organized in 1910 by rural South Carolinian schoolteacher Marie Samuella Cromer, she described the clubs as a means for members to "not learn simply how to grow better and more perfect tomatoes, but how to grow [into] better and more perfect women." Open to white and African American girls from 12 to 18 years old, principles were spread via Tomato

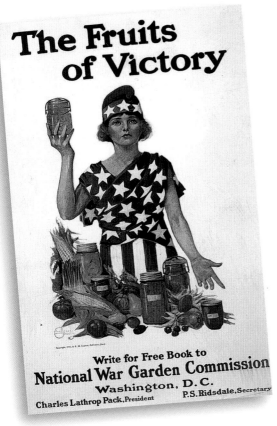

The Fruits of Victory

Write for Free Book to
National War Garden Commission
Washington, D.C.
Charles Lathrop Pack, President   P. S. Ridsdale, Secretary

In 1917, Charles Lathrop Pack organized the National War Garden Commission, urging the United States citizenry to plant war gardens in an effort to increase food supplies at home.

Circa 1910 to 1920, five members of the Vigo County Canning Club pose with the fruits of their war gardens.

Club agents who visited country schoolhouses. Prospective members were asked to cultivate one-tenth acre of land on which to plant tomatoes. For those who joined, harvest time would mean working in groups to can the outcome, which they would then sell. The girls would learn about food production, chemistry, and small business practices as well. Some might even earn scholarships if their crops performed well.

For many girls who joined, it was the first time they had money of their own—money they could choose to spend as they pleased. Some was allocated to the more frivolous—pretty dresses and the like—but many of the girls used their profits to reinvest in their businesses.

The first Tomato Clubs canned their harvests in tin or steel, which had to be soldered shut. This wasn't unusual for their consumers, who were accustomed to buying food in tins. Later, when profits permitted and pressure cookers became more readily available, girls invested in Mason jars in

which to can their produce. Soon, they planted *other* crops in their one-tenth acre. Their organization's moniker, "Tomato Club," no longer sufficed, and eventually became the more general "Canning Club."

Besides reinvesting in their businesses, the girls used their profits to invest in their futures, saving the money to further their educations. One girl, Margaret Brown, even offered to pay her tuition in canned goods to Raleigh's Peace Institute. We might easily assume that her temerity and salesmanship were in part a byproduct of her Tomato Club experiences.

Mason jars and moonshine

Even though Tomato Clubs and their subsequent Canning Clubs boosted Mason jars' popularity, it was the ratification of the 18th amendment in 1919 that really started things rolling. This time the unlikely demographic was moonshiners. During prohibition—also considered by many as "the golden age of moonshining"—these homegrown entrepreneurs saw the benefit of storing and selling their wares in Mason jars, as they provided a known quantity. A quart jar was a quart jar, no matter if it contained tomatoes or white lightning. From the imbiber's perspective, a Mason jar was a most fortuitous way to partake of moonshine, as the jar itself served as a communal glass that could be passed among friends.

So entwined are the histories of moonshine and Mason jars that several myths have blossomed from their union. First, it was said that moonshiners were so influential on the Mason jar business that companies like Ball manufactured square jars to be more packable. Another myth involves a 56-ounce jar that Ball manufactured that looked very much like a 64-ounce half-gallon jar. Contrary to Ball, the jar wasn't made in response to moonshiners' wishes to dupe their customers (although smart money would bet that some moonshiners did just that).

Still popular today is the myth of number 13. It's said that because of superstition, moonshiners would break Mason jars with the number 13 on the bottom. The "evidence" of this is the fact that today there are fewer Ball jars, and fruit jars in general, with the number 13 on the bottom. The numbers that appear on jars' bottoms refer to the individual jar's mold number. According to Ball, their machines had 8 to 10 molds apiece. Higher mold numbers only occurred when molds needed to be replaced, thereby generating a new number. Molds didn't need to be replaced that often, thus the true scarcity of the number 13 on the bottom of a Mason jar.

As the Great Depression began to settle in, fruit jar manufacturers took a hit. Moonshiners couldn't save them, but, ironically, it was their legal brethren in the hooch industry that did. On December 5, 1933, the country's failed experiment was repealed and liquor bottle sales soared. Although the Ball brothers, along with other glassmakers at the time, found their salvation, Frank Ball, possibly in deference to his teetotaling mother, insisted the liquor bottles they produce be called "flasks" or "special purpose bottles." Euphemisms aside, they held booze and Ball profited.

Mason jars and World War II

Jar manufacturers were ushered out of the Depression, like the rest of the country, with the onset of World War II. The supply of comestibles dwindled as a large portion of processed food, including products that were commercially canned, was being shipped overseas to feed the troops. Gasoline and tires were rationed as well, as they were needed to transport war supplies, not food. Trains and trucks were diverted from transporting food for the same reason. And finally, things such as coffee and sugar were in short supply due to import restrictions.

Unlike during World War I, self-rationing of foodstuffs wasn't going to cut it this time. In 1942, the Office

In Washington, DC, on September 3, 1922, a group of police officers serving as a liquor squad pose with Mason jars filled with moonshine.

of Price Administration and Civilian Supply established a rationing system so those items that were in short supply could be shared more equitably. Every US citizen was issued ration books for things such as meat, cooking oil, and the aforementioned coffee and sugar. Each book contained stamps, or coupons, that consumers had to surrender to grocers before they could buy the rationed item.

Along with the rationing of food came the Victory Garden. Across the country, people—even without gardens—started growing food.

From yards to rooftops to window boxes, people found places to farm. It's said that by 1944, 40 percent of the vegetables consumed in the United

Circa 1943, a grocer stores surrendered sugar and coffee ration stamps in Mason jars.

States were a product of these very gardens. Raising produce, and then canning it for later consumption, was regarded as a means to win the war. Gardeners and canners were patriots.

Further evidence of the success of the Victory Garden could be seen in the popularity of pressure cookers. An indispensable tool for the home canning enthusiast, sales of the cookers skyrocketed. In 1942, their sales in the

Poster championing the Victory Garden by the Stecher-Traung Lithograph Corporation, Rochester, New York, circa 1939 to 1945.

Circa 1940, Mrs. Marinus Hanson overlooks a fraction of the 500-plus quarts of fruit and vegetables she cans yearly.

United States were pegged at 66,000. Just a year later, in 1943, that number jumped to 315,000.

The Mason jar today

As the nation entered the race to the moon, home canning fell out of favor. People wanted TV dinners and Tang. In the 1950s, refrigerators were no longer a luxury item. Deep freezers, too, were finally affordable, and every suburb had a corner grocery store. The glory days of fruit jar production were over, but that didn't mean Mason jars disappeared.

Nor will they. Home canning has experienced a rebirth in recent years, thanks to the eat-local food movement, and clever crafters are finding new ways to use them every day. As for the collectors, they will carry the jars and their histories forward for years to come.

Longlife Mason jar manufactured by Obear-Nester Glass Company.

Collecting Jars

Do you own a Mason jar or two? Would you like to add to your collection? If so, you'll want to brush up on your jar identification skills. There are a myriad of ways to advance your Mason education, but we'll start with some quick and easy tips that can help you identify the era in which a jar was manufactured.

First, we'll need a short primer on how jars were actually made. Early fruit jars were hand-blown by a glassmaker using a blow pipe. When the basic jar shape was complete, it was transferred to an iron pontil rod that had been dipped into a small amount of hot glass. The hot glass on the pontil held the bottle in place as the glassmaker finished the neck of the jar by hand. When removed from the pontil rod, a ring of glass or a reddish-black mark remained on the bottom of the jar. This is called a "pontil scar." If you should be so lucky as to find a jar with such an identifier, you can be pretty sure that the jar predates 1855.

Wax sealers—jars stoppered with a cork and then sealed over with wax—had their heyday too. Although they have patent dates that reach back to the mid-1850s, the bulk of their creation occurred between the 1860s and 1890s.

Mold seams, too, can help determine a jar's age. Those early glassmakers that free-blew jars didn't use molds to create their shapes. Therefore, if a jar lacks mold seams, it's most likely older than one that *does* have body mold seams. Next oldest would be a jar that has a seam that runs up to its top/neck/lip. This jar was most likely blown into a mold and then its top/neck/lip was finished by hand. And, finally, the newest of the bunch would be jars with a body mold seam that runs up the side *including* the top/neck/lip, which would have been made sometime after 1915, when the glass-blowing industry started to be mechanized. We can thank Michael J. Owens for this, as he invented—and perfected—the first automatic bottle-making machine.

Early jar making was a multiple-man operation. In this picture, taken in October of 1908 in Wheeling, West Virginia, a glass blower and "mold boy" work in tandem.

With the advent of machine-made jars came the "bead seal," which consisted of a bead of glass placed just below the threads on the jar's neck. A replacement for the old Mason shoulder seal, the bead seal was a more durable closure and was not affected as much by pressure. Therefore, if a jar has a bead seal, we can estimate that it was also made sometime after 1915.

Now a word about color. Want to pique a collector's interest? Say the words olive green, amethyst, or cornflower blue and see what happens. Experienced and novice fruit jar collectors alike love color. And, lucky for us, color is a good way to determine a jar's age.

The basic formula to make glass is pretty simple—sand, soda, and lime. The naturally occurring color outcome of the mix is aqua, which is dependent upon the amount of iron in the sand used. However, around the turn of the twentieth century public interest started gravitating to clear glass, as clear glass implied purity.

Glassmakers knew that adding manganese to their sand/soda/lime mix would decolorize glass, and from 1880 to about 1915, that's what they used if they wanted to produce a clear product. But when World War I broke out, glassmakers' German source of manganese was cut off. They had to find another decolorizing agent, which was selenium.

Unbeknownst to glassmakers at the time, the decolorizing agents added to the recipe reacted in a most magical way when exposed to ultraviolet light. If the glass contained manganese, it turned light amethyst when exposed to the sun; if it contained selenium, it turned light yellow.

The jar on the left has a rough ground lip and shoulder seal. The jar on the right has a smooth machined lip and a bead seal.

So using everything we know about history, glassmaking, and a tiny bit of chemistry, we can peg jars that have an amethyst hue to predate the onset of World War I. Jars that have a yellow hue postdate the onset of World War I.

Early glass manufacturers used manganese to make glass clear. Exposed to sunlight, glass containing this chemical turns light amethyst. The onset of World War I cut off the nation's supply of manganese, which came from Germany. Glass manufacturers then turned to selenium to clarify glass, which causes glass to turn light yellow when exposed to sunlight. Because the Mason jars pictured here have turned amethyst, we can assume they were made prior to World War I.

The recent popularity of Mason jars—especially colorful ones—and advancements in science have converged in a disturbing trend, however. Unscrupulous dealers sometimes take advantage of the manganese in old, clear jars and subject them to either extreme heat or radiation—a process called irradiating—causing them to change color. The effect can be subtle, but more often than not, the effects are extreme, turning the once-clear glass into a deep purple or even muddy brown. Of course, the jars' unnatural transformation when undergoing the irradiating process compromises not only their material integrity, but also the integrity of historical bottles and glassware as well. When the glass is irradiated, its history is interrupted and diverges into one of profit making, which in and of itself could be seen as another chapter in fruit jar history. For now, however, these altered jars confuse the would-be collector, presenting color extremes that would not have occurred naturally.

Although sun-colored jars were a serendipitous result of adding decolorizing agents, some makers chose to intentionally color their glass from the outset. Take amber, for instance. To produce glass of this hue, manufacturers would add carbon or nickel to their sand/soda/lime glass recipe. The impetus for making amber or brown jars was the opinion that such colors would keep fruit from turning dark. The jars' consumers, however, disagreed; they bristled at the fact that they couldn't see the contents when the jars were filled.

Sometimes, at the end of a day's work, glassmakers would throw whatever leftovers they had on hand into the mix. The outcome produced colorful—and highly collectible—results. From cobalt to sky blue, from straw yellow to black amber, from emerald green to teal, from dark olive to amber olive, an assemblage of colorful jars can look like a big box of crayons.

No discussion about fruit jar colors would be complete without mentioning Ball blue. When the Ball brothers moved their operations to Muncie, Indiana, in 1887, they needed sand to make their glass jars. Their attention turned to the Hoosier Slide sand dune near Michigan City.

A collection of general store canning jars. Note the sun-colored amethyst jar on the top row, third from the left.

Fortuitously, the 200-foot mountain of sand held just the right amount of iron to make that unmistakable aqua blue. Along with other glass manufacturers, Ball mined the Hoosier Slide to extinction. By 1920, the sand was gone but the Ball brothers had enough in their reserves to last another decade. Therefore, most Ball blue jars were produced from 1900 to 1930, and by about 1937, the last jars in this color were made.

Ball has made other colorful jars in the past 40 years, but all have been designated as commemorative. In 1976, they released a replica amber Buffalo Jar, and in 2013 they announced their Heritage Collection, which celebrated the 100th anniversary of their Perfect Mason iteration. Colors in the Heritage Collection include green, purple, and blue.

Continuing with Ball, the time has come to talk about the company's embossed logos as a factor in jar dating. The jars' ages can be estimated by examining certain defining features. The oldest and rarest of the Ball jar family is the amber Buffalo Jar, manufactured from 1885 to 1886; its most recognizable feature, besides its amber color, is its stacked BBGM CO logo. The next inception of Ball jars, from 1895 to 1896, sports a simple "BALL" moniker in all-capital block letters. The first Ball logo that is in cursive letters also dates from 1895 to 1896 and is underlined. From 1900 to 1910, the embossed "Ball" appears to have a third "l" that extends *into* the underline. (These are what collectors refer to as "Ball-y jars.") From 1910 to 1923, the "a" in "Ball" is down-stroked and the third "l" has been removed. From 1923 to 1933, the cursive remains but the underline is eliminated. The underline returns from 1933 to 1962. While Ball was still manufacturing jars

A 1976 reproduction of a Ball Brothers Glass Manufacturing Company "Buffalo Jar." Even as a reproduction, these jars are prized by collectors.

A selection of vintage Ball jars still readily available for purchase. They're pictured oldest—a Ball-y jar—to youngest. The embossing has been highlighted with a white latex paint pen. Collectors often highlight their jars' embossings with latex paint to make them easier to identify at a glance. It's also easier to photograph highlighted embossing for online sales and inventorying purposes.

with this logo design, they also began producing jars that feature a closed "B"; these date from 1960 to 1976. A registered trademark symbol (®) is added in 1976 and remains today. If all that sounds complicated, it really isn't, especially when you accumulate a jar or two and start comparing them.

Although these tips will help you gauge a jar's approximate age and scarcity, the best way to identify both age and maker of a fruit jar is to consult an expert. First, we turn to books. Considered a bible of sorts in fruit jar collecting is Alice Creswick's *The Fruit Jar Works*, volumes I and II. Ms. Creswick's extensive work includes descriptions (with illustrations done

by her husband, Howard Creswick) as well as manufacturing information and creation dates. The Creswick books are out of print but can be found on the secondary market for a premium price.

Also out of print yet much more affordable is the aforementioned *Fruit Jars* by Julian Harrison Toulouse. Mr. Toulouse's book leans heavily on the historical aspects of fruit jars, such as their makers, individual patent chronologies, and sealing methods, the last of which is a fascinating history unto itself.

The third in the holy trinity of fruit jar books is Dick Roller's *The Standard Fruit Jar Reference*, which is also out of print but can be found on the used market.

Honorable mention needs to go to Cecil Munsey's *Collecting Bottles*. Although it is not fruit jar specific, Mr. Munsey's historical knowledge about glassmaking, and glass bottle collecting in general, is immeasurable, including his research devoted to glass molds, empontilling, and decolorizing, all of which help in dating and, therefore, determining collectibility of bottles and jars.

Possibly the most invaluable tool in dating jars is to ask other, more experienced collectors. You can find such people on jar-collecting websites that have an active online community. Post a picture of the jar under consideration and your inquiry on their message board, and you're sure to get a response. For total immersion, visit historical glass and bottle shows, where the attendees' wealth of knowledge will be unprecedented. You can find a list of upcoming shows by visiting The Federation of Historical Bottle Collectors' webpage, www.fohbc.org/shows. (The most notable show dedicated to fruit jars occurs annually in Muncie, Indiana.)

An added benefit of going to a historical glass and bottle show is that the collectors there will be selling jars with which they are willing to part company. Some may call these their less desirable (AKA cheaper) jars, but don't let that dissuade you from buying. To a newbie, their undesirable stuff is very desirable. Trust me. And, although this might come as a surprise, the deals to be had at a jar show can be very attractive. Many collectors have over-collected and just want to cull the herd or sell off to make some cash to buy something more collectible (AKA expensive). They're usually not looking to turn a great profit. They just want a fair price, which serves to everyone's advantage and carries on the tradition of collecting.

Although going to shows is elucidating and entertaining, it's best to start looking for jars locally—very locally, like in grandma's attic or basement. Then take your hunt toyard sales, thrift shops, estate sales, and auctions.

Jars you find in such places might be dirty or have a distinctive haze, either inside or outside. For these situations, a damp cloth kept in a small plastic zip-top bag can be very handy. Swiping the cloth over the jar is a good way to see if the haze is just dirt or something else. If the damp cloth doesn't remove the haze, it could have been permanently etched by its former contents. That doesn't mean the particular jar isn't worthy of your money. Very old jars are not going to look like they came straight from a blower's pipe. In fact, they look quite crude. However, haze *can* be a factor in pricing, especially in newer jars.

When you feel ready, antique stores—both brick-and-mortar and virtual—can offer up some lovely specimens. These jars will consistently be in better shape than those found in yard sales and the like, but keep in

A collection of vintage jars I've found at local thrift stores. Each cost $1 a piece, with the exception of the blue pint-size Ball jar, which set me back $3.

mind that prices can vary widely from shop to shop and listing to listing.

Online auctions are another avenue to explore, but, like buying from a virtual antique shop, it's best to have some vintage jar knowledge before bidding on an item. That way, you'll know what questions to ask the seller and what to look for in the posted pictures. Because you can't physically examine the item, always proceed with caution in such circumstances.

Handling a jar before you buy it, if you can, is imperative. Always remove its lid, if it has one, and check for chipping, which usually occurs around the mouth of a jar. Again, chips can diminish a jar's collectibility.

If the jar doesn't have a lid, don't worry. You can always search for that later. Remember, for the first 20-plus years, lids and jars weren't sold together, and antique stores always seem to have a stash of extra lids somewhere.

On one excursion to an antique store, I met a dealer who was selling her (now grown) son's fruit jar collection. She said he had started accumulating them as a little boy because they were an affordable collectible. The same could be said today. Prices on vintage fruit jars have increased, to be sure, but it's still possible to find a nice quart-size blue Ball jar with a conventional threaded

zinc lid or lightning closure for about the same price as a couple of fancy coffee drinks. Which means, although they may hold great sentimental value, those blue Ball jars in grandma's basement or attic might not be worth as much as we think. We can thank the prodigious manufacturing of the Ball brothers for that. Remember, they made a lot of them—75 million in 1905 alone.

But what about the *really* rare stuff, the stuff that will make you jump for joy? That would be anything with an error—jars with misspelled words. (Ball "error" jars include PERFFCT, PEPRECT, and PEREFCT, to name just a few.) Jars embossed with backward letters or images can demand a high price. Jars with overly complicated wire-and-bail, spring-clamp closures can make a collector swoon. Jars that are equivalent to winning the lottery would include one of those "made under the auspices of John L. Mason" jars, a jar made in the time of Appert, and the extraordinarily rare Ball amber Buffalo Jar.

This being said, pricing jars is next to impossible for an amateur and can still be tricky for the seasoned collector. Unless you're Douglas M. Leybourne, that is. One might call Mr. Leybourne the chronicler of fruit jar pricing. He documents his findings in his publication entitled, *Red Book: The Collector's Guide to Old Fruit Jars*. Known simply as "The Red Book" to collectors, its latest iteration's number is 11 and can be found by visiting Mr. Leyborne's website, www.redbookjars.com.

Vintage square jars are generally priced a bit higher than their round counterparts of the same age.

So what makes a jar collectible *besides* color and age? Any jar embossed with the Mason 1858 patent date fetches a few dollars more than the average Ball of the same vintage. Square jars, which were made as a means to store more compactly in cupboards and root cellars and such, are priced a bit higher than their round counterparts. General consensus suggests this is due to the fact that fewer were made. Also, the tinier the jar, the better. Half-pint jars are oftentimes priced at a premium over larger sizes of the same brand.

Now that we know a little bit about what jars to look for and where, how should we begin our collections? Collecting Mason jars for Mason jars' sake can quickly become overwhelming. A Ball jar here, an Atlas jar there, and soon your collection will be collecting you and not vice versa. Therefore, it's best to specialize—as does my friend John, whose focus is on unusual closures.

Other ideas for collections might be amassing square jars, or jars in sets—from half-pint to half-gallon— with lightning closures or otherwise. Mason jars with the 1858 patent date might make for a lovely collection. Wax sealers would be worthy of your time, as would jars with #13 embossed on the bottom. The latter may have an inflated value based upon moonshine mythology, but they are still rare in and of themselves.

As you collect, your interests may expand and include fruit jar "go-withs," like jar wrenches, vintage pressure canners, shipping boxes, and advertising.

You never know where that first jar in your collection will take you.

For further information on fruit jars and fruit jar collecting, there is a wealth of information at your fingertips, thanks to the Internet. A good place to start is reading the very informative article "A Primer on Fruit Jars," by Dave Hinson, at www.av.qnet.com/~glassman/info/b&e/primer.htm as well as his "Frequently Asked Questions— Fruit Jars" article at www.av.qnet.com/~glassman/info/jarfaq.htm. Next, a visit to the Midwest Antique Fruit Jar & Bottle Club at www.fruitjar.org is recommended, as is a detour to Collectors Weekly (www.collectorsweekly.com, search "fruit jars"). A plethora of information about jars and bottles in general can be found on The Federation of Historical Bottle Collectors website (www.fohbc.org). For Ball-specific history, visit Minnetrista (www.minnetrista.net), and to watch an engaging documentary about the Ball family and corporation, entitled "A Legacy Etched in Glass," visit www.vimeo.com/96710414. And finally, the Society of Historical Archaeology is a remarkable resource containing exhaustive amounts of information concerning all aspects of glass jars and glassmaking—from colors to closures to seams and everything in between; visit them by going to www.sha.org/bottle/index.htm.

Technical Information

You've probably handled, or even own most of the supplies used to make the Mason jar projects included in the next section. But for the more, shall we say, *adventurous* tutorials, you'll need to break out some hand tools. In the following pages, I'll cover the most important ones, along with my recommendations as to the tools themselves and to the finishing processes.

MAKING HOLES IN MASON JAR
·········· LIDS AND BANDS ··········

First, let's talk safety. When drilling or cutting tin lids and bands, *always* wear gloves and eye protection. I prefer wearing leather or leather–like gloves, as they provide the best protection against sharp tin edges.

For the projects in *Mason Jar Nation* that require making holes in Mason jar lids or bands, most people will likely grab a drill to get the job done. If you do it this way, you'll need to clamp the lid to a scrap piece of lumber, then punch a hole in the lid with a hammer and nail so the drill bit doesn't walk. Be aware, this method very often produces a ragged edge that will definitely need

To prevent tear-back, sandwich the lid between two scrap pieces of wood before drilling.

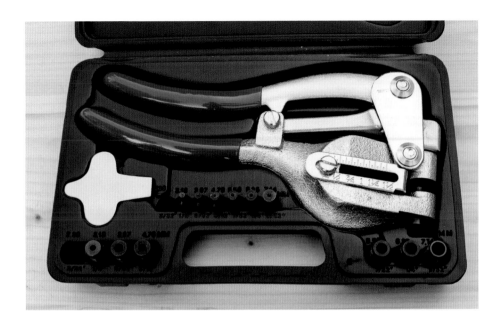

An inexpensive metal hole-punch kit.

to be deburred, especially if drilling holes greater than ¼" in diameter. That's because as the drill bit breaks through the thin material, it pulls the metal up.

A better way to produce a less jagged hole when using a drill and bit is to support both sides of the lid by sandwiching it between two pieces of wood. To do this, first drill a hole in a waste piece of wood. Then align the hole in the scrap wood over the punched mark on the lid. Clamp them both to another piece of scrap wood and drill through the hole in the wood, then through the lid and into the waste wood below.

A great alternative to using a drill and bit is to invest in an inexpensive metal hole punch. Metal hole punches generally come in kits that include interchangeable dies that punch varying sizes of holes.

The nice thing about these handy tools is that they produce clean, virtually burr-free holes exactly where you want them. They're also more versatile than you might imagine, as they can be used to punch holes into plastic, cardboard, and even card stock.

Punching a perfect hole in a jar lid with a metal hole punch.

DRILL WITH SANDWICH METHOD

DRILL BIT ONLY

METAL PUNCH

Starting at the lower left and working clockwise, holes made using a drill and bit, a drill and bit using the sandwich method, and, finally, using a metal punch. Note the edges of each.

If making very large holes in jar lids, you can dispense with a drill and bit altogether. That's because the material is so thin that it can be cut with small, sharp utility scissors. Simply start by drilling a pilot hole—to get the point of the scissors through—in the center of the lid, then snip away.

Drilling a hole in a jar band lip.

You can cut larger holes in jar lids using a sharp utility scissors.

Because the material thickness in rings/bands is greater than that of jar lids, it means less tear-back, so both drill and punch work equally well when making holes in the threaded area of the jar bands. But, once again, the punch will produce a cleaner, more precisely located hole. As for speed, that's no contest. The punch will win every time.

Where the drill excels over the punch is at the very tops of the jar rings/bands, as it's virtually impossible to punch a hole in that small lip.

CUTTING JARS

Again, let's talk safety first. When cutting jars, *always* wear gloves and eye protection. I prefer wearing leather or leather-like gloves when scoring jars as they provide protection and grip.

Leather or leather-like gloves provide protection against sharp metal edges and cut glass.

Two popular bottle cutters currently on the market.

When sanding the jars' cut edges, which I do underwater, I switch to waterproof gardening gloves because they provide protection and grip.

For additional safety precautions, *always* consult the instructions included with your metal punch and bottle cutter.

As far as bottle cutters go, there's quite a selection on the market to choose from, but the most user-friendly are those with horizontal beds. Two horizontal models currently on the market are pictured below left.

It may come as a surprise to some, but bottle cutters don't actually cut bottles—they score them. Through a process of heating and cooling, which we'll discuss later, the bottles break—or separate—on their scored lines.

All bottle cutters will require a learning curve, so you'll want to practice with jars and bottles salvaged

Note where the scoring wheel lands. The jar is positioned so the wheel avoids the embossing when the jar is rotated.

from the recycling bin. Remove their labels and all label adhesive before you attempt to score them. Only after you have the scoring and separating technique down should you try to attempt cutting more desirable jars.

When it's finally time to score a Mason jar, the most important thing to keep in mind is to *avoid embossing*! Neither the scoring wheel nor the rollers on the cutting bed will roll smoothly over heavily embossed jars. This invariably leads to wobbly score lines and ragged separation lines—if the jars separate at all. Ball jars, vintage or contemporary, have notoriously heavy-handed embossing. Contemporary Kerr jars, on the other hand, have less embossing. And what embossing they do have isn't as prominent as that on jars such as Ball. For this reason, go with contemporary Kerr jars when you first start cutting jars. And although they have much less character, another

even better alternative for beginners is using quart-size "smooth" Mason jars that have no embossing.

One way to separate two halves of a cut jar is to slowly rotate its score line above a candle flame, then follow it up by pouring cold water evenly along the score line.

SEPARATING AND FINISHING
·········· CUT JARS ··········

As mentioned earlier, you don't actually cut bottles. You score them and then separate them. The secret to producing a good separation is dependent upon producing a good score line. To accomplish the latter, we already know to *avoid embossing*, but you shouldn't overscore either. One steady and even turn over the scoring wheel is all you should need to make a clean score line.

Once you confirm your score line is continuous and even, it will be time to separate the two halves. The instructions included in your bottle

An even score line on a practice jar ready for separation.

Always sand cut jars while they are fully submerged in water and while wearing protective waterproof gloves!

cutter packaging will provide directions on how to do this, but two popular methods will be discussed here.

One way to separate a jar is with *hot* water evenly poured along the score line followed by *cold* water evenly poured along the score line. Another method that I've used successfully is slowly rotating the jar's score line above a candle flame, then following it up by pouring cold water evenly along the score line. Whichever way you choose to separate the jars, it will require practice.

You may have heard that the most tedious part of cutting a jar or bottle is finishing the cut edge. If you use the right tools, it doesn't have to be.

The secret to a fast and smooth finish is in the type of sandpaper you use; I strongly recommend the *silicon carbide* variety. That's because silicon carbide sandpaper can stand up to both glass and water. Why water? Because

you'll want to sand your glass *underwater* (a bucket works great for this) to prevent inhalation of silica dust.

When finishing cut edges of bottles to make drinking glasses, a common procedure is to start with an 80-grit silicon carbide sandpaper and move up to paper with increasingly finer grit to produce a smooth, lip-friendly edge. But, for the projects in this book, I stopped at 80-grit, as I felt it provided a sufficient and safe finish.

·············· OTHER HANDY TIPS ··············

When working with Mason jars, keep a bottle brush nearby for cleaning them. You only have to get your hand stuck inside a jar once to learn your lesson here.

To get labels off jars, soaking in hot water is usually all that's needed. If glue residue remains, it can be removed with various commercial products such as mineral spirits, Goo Gone, or, my favorite, Citra Solv.

Remember, just because a jar doesn't say "Mason" on it doesn't make it any less worthy of one of the

projects in *Mason Jar Nation*. Actually, using generic jars—for example, glass mayonnaise jars—is perfect for practicing a new technique such as etching or cutting.

And, finally, some of the projects you'll come across in the next pages involve cutting wood. For brevity's sake, I've stipulated using a table saw or handsaw in the instructions, but other saws—like a power miter saw and a band saw, for instance—could work just as well.

The Projects

With the exception of those things that require a medical degree, we're up for just about any kind of DIY in my house. Sometimes I'm knee-deep in the joyful mess of making things, but sometimes I'm the cheerleader on the sidelines or the one handing off the tools. "Nurse, impact driver, *stat!*" I'm cool with any and all roles in a DIY operation. Which brings me to the projects you'll see over the next 100 pages of *Mason Jar*

Nation. Although I can't be there to hand you the instruments you'll need to make them, I will be there in spirit, cheering you on and standing beside you in the joyful mess of making things.

Hanging Air Plant Planter

Educated types will tell you that tillandsia, also known as "air plants," are epiphytes. No need to remember that, as there isn't going to be a quiz at the end of this project. What you do need to know is that epiphytes don't require dirt to grow. They siphon the nutrients they need from the air, and, as for watering, a one-hour dunk every couple of weeks or a spritz every couple of days is just what the horticulturist ordered. The best water to use is of the rain variety, of course, but distilled works well, as does tap water that's been sitting for 12 hours "off-gassing." For sunlight, these virtually indestructible darlings prefer that which is bright filtered. Tillandsia's unique growing requirements make them the perfect plants to grow in Mason jars.

Supplies

• 1 clear, quart-size Mason jar • Bottle cutter and finishing equipment • Painter's tape • Small paintbrush • Etching cream • Metal hole punch or drill and small bit • 1 lid and band or 1 reproduction lid to fit the Mason jar used • 1 small cotter pin • 2' of #16 single jack electro-galvanized chain • Small washer with a small hole • 18-gauge wire (about 8" or so) • 1 tillandsia

MAKING YOUR PLANTER

1. Cut approximately 1" off the bottom of the jar and finish the cut edge according to the technical instructions in this book (p. 35–36) or according to the bottle cutter's instructions.

2. Apply painter's tape about ½" up from bottom edge of jar.

3. With a small paintbrush, apply etching cream to the exposed area. A thick, even coat works best. Leave the etching cream in place for as long as the product's recommendations stipulate. After that, rinse off the etching cream and remove the tape.

4. Next, punch or drill a small hole in the jar's lid. Thread the cotter pin through the last link in the chain, then feed the cotter pin's legs through the hole in the lid. Slip the washer onto the cotter pin's legs and bend them open.

5. Using a length of 18-gauge wire, gently wire up the tillandsia. Then feed one end of the wire through the top of the jar and screw on the jar's lid.

6. When it's time to water the tillandsia, remove the lid and ease the plant out. Allow it to dry before re-inserting it into the jar.

Music Box
Memory Jar

G o into any thrift store and, invariably, you'll be met with more than a few seen-better-days music boxes. Some might even be snow globes having suffered climate change—you know, when half the water has mysteriously escaped from the inside? Luckily, this project doesn't care what the music box looks like. The only thing that's important is that it sounds lovely and that its musical insides are easy to get at. Most likely, the movement will be held in place by a couple of small screws. Maybe even a bit of glue. But that's not going to stop us from turning a Mason jar into a Music Box Memory Jar.

Supplies

- 1 thrifted music box that sounds lovely • A small screwdriver, straight or Phillips, depending upon the construction of the music box • Paper or lightweight cardboard • Pencil • Scissors • 1 lid and band or 1 reproduction lid to fit the Mason jar used • Metal punch or a drill with a bit large enough to fit the music box screws and turnkey stem • 1 Mason jar with a mouth large enough to fit the music box movement • Sentimental things to put inside the jar

MAKING YOUR MUSIC JAR

1. First, a little deconstruction. Unscrew the turnkey, also known as the windup key, by turning it—usually counterclockwise. Remove the screws from the bottom of the music box and lift out the musical movement. Remember to save the screws!

2. With a piece of paper or lightweight cardboard, make a template of the musical movement where the screws and turnkey holes are located. Transfer the template to the jar's lid and drill or punch holes in the lid to match the template.

3. Line up the holes in the movement to the holes in the jar.

4. Attach the movement with the screws you saved during deconstruction and screw on the turnkey.

5. Fill the jar with happy memories. For this jar, that's sand, a picture of a favorite destination, and miniatures that relate to it. A little bauble to decorate the jar's band, and it's done. (You're wondering what music my jar is playing, aren't you? It's "Unchained Melody.")

Mason Jar
Cloche

Gardeners have been familiar with cloches, or bell jars, for centuries. Traditionally, they were used to incubate seedlings and to protect young plants from inclement weather, acting as miniature greenhouses. (*Cold snap coming? Pop on a cloche!*) But somewhere along the home decor history timeline, they moved indoors as well. Now, glass bell jars are used to protect and highlight collectibles more often than veggies. Mason jars, especially non-embossed ones, make lovely little cloches for a fraction of the cost of the ready-made variety, and they couldn't be easier to construct.

Supplies

• 2 quart-size non-embossed Mason jar • Bottle cutter
and finishing equipment • 1 jar lid and band or a reproduction
lid to fit the Mason jar used • 1 small drawer pull,
3/4" in diameter • Craft glue, such as E6000
• Spray paint (oil-rubbed bronze was used in this project)
• *Optional:* round, flat surface, such as a piece of wood, plate,
or stone hot pad slightly larger in diameter than the jar

MAKING YOUR CLOCHE

1. Cut approximately 1" off the bottom of the jar and finish the cut edge according to the technical instructions in this book (p. 35–36) or according to the bottle cutter's instructions.

2. Glue the drawer pull to the top center of the jar lid with craft glue. If using a band and lid combination, glue the lid to the band as well.

3. When the glue is dry, spray-paint the entire lid assembly.

4. Although having a round surface to set your cloche upon isn't necessary, it's a nice finishing touch to the project.

Concrete Mason
Jar Lid

It's the nineteenth century. Mechanical engineer William Ward wants to build his family a new home, but he is deathly afraid of fire. Such a fear isn't unreasonable in a time when open flames are used for survival. Lighting, cooking, and heating coupled with combustibles that are commonplace in every household can make even the bravest among us skittish. But William Ward isn't just any mechanical engineer. Oh, no. He is a forward-thinking mechanical engineer who knows a thing or two about concrete. With the help of friend and architect Robert Mook, Ward builds a reinforced concrete home in Port Chester, New York. Completed in 1875, it is the first of its kind in the United States.

The fireproof home was first mockingly referred to as "Ward's Folly" because of prognostications that it was just a matter of time before the house collapsed under its own weight. Still standing sound and looking much as it did when first constructed, today the building is known as "Ward's Castle." So much for the naysayers.

Mr. Ward's creation marked the turning point in the country for modern uses of concrete. From impenetrable facades to highly prized interior decor elements, such as flooring and countertops, concrete is everywhere. And now, it's even topping a Mason jar.

Supplies

- An empty, plastic cylindrical container slightly larger than the jar band (an empty cake frosting container works perfectly) • Utility scissors or tin snips • Craft glue, such as E6000 • 1 lid and band to fit the jar • Empty container in which to mix the concrete • Water • 1 cup of Portland cement • Cooking spray • A few pebbles for weight • 1 Mason jar with a regular-size opening

MAKING YOUR CONCRETE LID

1. Cut down the edges of the frosting container so it's approximately 2" tall. This will become the mold for the concrete mix.

2. Glue the jar lid and band together with craft glue. Let dry.

3. In the other empty container, mix clean water to 1 cup of Portland cement until reaching the consistency stipulated on the product's packaging.

4. Spray cooking spray inside the mold. Fill the mold with approximately 1" of mixed concrete.

5. Nestle the lid assembly into the mold, displacing the concrete. Stack pebbles inside the lid just until the band's edge is equal to the top of the concrete.

6. After the concrete has cured, coax the entire part out of the mold, and twist the new lid onto the Mason jar.

Mason Jar Vase Frog

*W*hy are flower frogs called frogs? No one knows—although we can speculate that they acquired the moniker because they look like frogs squatting inside vases. That might not sound decorative, but they were. They were also seen as a handy tool for floral arranging, to keep stems exactly where the arranger intended. Nowadays, many people contend that flower frogs are unnecessary. They're right. With enough of the right kinds of flowers, and some flower-arranging talent, you don't need them. But what if you want to use the *wrong* kinds of flowers? Like those of the posy variety, whose short, delicate stems aren't conducive to arranging? In that case, a Mason jar frog is just the ticket.

Supplies

- 1 band to fit the opening of the jar used • Felt-tip pen
- Translucent plastic container lid from the recycling bin
- Utility scissors • Hole punch (a regular paper hole punch will work just fine) • 1 Mason jar with either a wide- or regular-mouth opening (the half-pint or 4-ounce size jars are particularly nice for this project)

MAKING YOUR VASE FROG

1. Use the jar band to trace a circle with a felt-tip pen onto the plastic container lid. Cut out the circle.

2. Punch random, or not so random, holes into the lid.

3. Fit the lid inside the band and twist onto the jar. Arrange posies as desired.

Note: A benefit of using a translucent plastic container lid, versus the jar lid itself, is that it virtually disappears underneath the blossoms of your flowers. Another plus is the edges of the punched holes are gentle against the delicate stems of your flowers while keeping them from toppling out of the vase.

Glamorous Place Setting Favors

Nicholas

Canning took a glamorous turn in the 1960s. It was then that the Ball Company introduced fruit jars that had a quilted texture. Dubbed GlamourGlas when it first appeared in advertising copy, the jars were a modern, compact twist on an old favorite. They were said to be pretty enough to grace a table and fancy enough for gifting homemade preserves. For this project, they're doing both: acting as decorative place settings and party favors.

Supplies

- 4-ounce quilted canning jars with matching bands and lids, one per place setting • Colorful scrapbook paper
- White card stock or printer paper • Marking pen or pencil
- Scissors • Computer printer (optional)
- White craft glue • A tasty treat to put inside the jars

MAKING YOUR PLACE SETTINGS

1. Using one of the jars' lids as a template, mark and cut a circle out of the scrapbook paper. You'll need one circle for each place setting, of course.

2. Write each guest's name on a slip of paper, or, if you're like me and suffer from a fear of hand lettering, use your computer and a pleasing font to do the work for you. Print the list of names onto card stock and cut them out to fit the diameter of the lids.

3. Center the names inside the paper circles, gluing them into place.

4. Fill the Mason jars with treats. Sandwich the scrapbook paper circles between the jar lids and bands and twist them onto the jars.

Lucky Bamboo
Water Garden

Before we jump into this project, let's talk stalks. The number of bamboo stalks you add to your lucky bamboo water garden is very important in feng shui circles. One symbolizes simplicity; two, love and harmony; three, happiness; five, achievement and creativity; seven, health; eight, wealth; nine, luck and good fortune in every aspect of life; and ten, fulfillment and excellence. Any more than that will most likely require a different vessel.

Numbers aren't the only things we might want to keep in mind when making our lucky bamboo water gardens. To increase their potency, we can add representatives of each of the five elements, those being wood (the plant itself), fire (something red), earth (rocks), metal (a Mason jar ring), and water. With all the symbols in mind, we can now get down to business.

Supplies

- 1 wide-mouth jar band • Marking pen • Scrap wood
- Drill and tiny bit • Sewing needle
- 40" of red pearl cotton or embroidery thread
- One 1-pint, wide-mouth Mason jar • Aquarium gravel or rocks • 1 or more lucky bamboo stalks • Distilled water

MAKING YOUR GARDEN

1. Mark 12 evenly spaced holes around the inside top of the jar band. Place the band on a piece of scrap wood, and drill a tiny hole at each of the markings.

2. Thread the needle with the pearl cotton or embroidery thread. Bring the thread up through a hole in the band. (We're going to consider this hole #1.) Count over to hole #5 and bring the thread through it. Then count over to hole #9 and bring the thread through it. Take the thread back over to hole #1 to complete a triangle.

3. Carry the thread from hole #1 to hole #2 and repeat the process that you used creating the first triangle, this time moving from hole #2 to hole #6 to hole #10 and so on until you've used all 12 holes made in the lid.

4. Secure the ends of your thread by making a knot close to the holes on the underside of the band, and trim the excess thread.

5. Fill your jar with about 2" of rocks, nestle the bamboo stalks into them, and slip the stalks and leaves through the center of the red starburst.

6. Add water, which should be changed weekly. Place your bamboo garden in bright, indirect light.

Kids' Activity
Jars

ack in the nineteenth century, the word "unplug" was used in one of two ways: to remove a plug or stopper, or to free an obstruction. Our Victorian ancestors could never have guessed that, a handful of generations later, "unplug" would also refer to removing oneself from electronic distraction.

Nowadays, we could all do with a little digital downtime every now and then. Adults, yes—but children too. The kiddos might be the trickiest to wean off the Wi-Fi, which is why this project is tailored especially to them. I like to keep these jars handy when kids come to visit, because not only does it help them from getting bored, but they can unplug while having fun.

Supplies

• 3 half-gallon, wide-mouth Mason jars,
1 for each age group • 3 plastic wide-mouth
one-piece lids • Washi tape • Toys!

MAKING YOUR ACTIVITY JARS

1. The most time-consuming—but also the most fun—thing about this project is accumulating the toys for the jars. When choosing toys, keep in mind their size; they have to fit through the jars' openings! Also keep in mind age-appropriateness, although there may be crossover. Here are some examples of the age groups and toys that you might consider:

For the five- to six-year-old:
• 24- to 54-piece puzzles (in a zippered bag)
• Card games such as Old Maid and Go Fish
• Small kaleidoscope
• Finger puppets

For the six- to seven-year-old:
• 54- to 100-piece puzzles (in a zippered bag)
• Standard playing cards with instructions for Snap and Crazy Eights
• Wooden tic-tac-toe board game
• Silly Putty

For the seven- to eight-year-old:
• Jacob's ladder
• Set of marbles or jacks
• Cat's Cradle string
• Standard playing cards with instructions for rummy

2. After the jars are filled, or even before, apply washi tape around the plastic lids for a fun finishing touch.

Tissue Paper
Tumblers

I t's said that Henry David Thoreau first wrote of feeding birds as a pastime in the pages of *Walden*. It took another 100 years for the popularity of attracting birds to backyards to begin in earnest. Ever since, armchair ornithologists have been hanging feeders from trees, beams, and shepherd's hooks. We can thank the less-appreciated barnyard variety of fowl—and HVAC parts—for making quick work of turning a Mason jar into a bird feeder.

Supplies

- One ³⁄₁₆" machine eyebolt and 2 nuts to fit • Hacksaw
- Drill and ¹⁄₈" bit • One 4" round galvanized steel vent cover
- Clear silicone caulk • 1 quart-size, regular-mouth Mason jar
- 1 poultry jar feeder, found at farm and garden stores
- Birdseed • #16 single jack electro-galvanized chain, optional

MAKING YOUR BIRD FEEDER

1. Hacksaw the bolt down to approximately ½".

2. Drill a ¹⁄₈" hole at the center of the vent cover; thread a nut onto the eyebolt; slip the eyebolt through the hole, and screw on the second nut.

3. Add a generous—and I mean *generous*—amount of silicone caulk to the bottom of the Mason jar, starting at the edge and working in.

4. Slip the end cap over the bottom of the jar.

5. Grab a tiny bit and drill a dozen or more weep holes into the bottom of the poultry feeder. When the caulk has cured, fill the jar with birdseed and twist the poultry feeder onto the jar. Invert the jar and hang from the eyebolt. To lengthen, add #16 single jack electro-galvanized chain to the eyebolt, if desired.

Mason Jar
Butterfly Feeder

I f honey bees and bumblebees are hero pollinators, butterflies are their indispensable sidekicks. These showy lepidopterans gracefully—and hypnotically—flit from flower to flower, adding color to the landscape they help create. Attracting them to our backyards is a gift to us and our gardens. And making their very own feeder—filled with homemade nectar—couldn't be easier.

Supplies

- Drill and ½" (or so) bit or metal punch • 1 regular-mouth Mason jar lid and band • Small piece of natural sponge • Scissors • 6' of yellow nylon cord • 1 large flat-topped silk flower (red, deep pink, or purple are good choices to attract butterflies) • Craft glue, such as E6000 • 1 pint-size, regular-mouth Mason jar • Painter's tape • Cooking pot and stove • Granulated sugar • Water

MAKING YOUR BUTTERFLY FEEDER

1. Punch or drill a ½" or so hole in the Mason jar lid. Cut a bit off the sponge and stuff it into the hole.

2. Cut two pieces of the nylon cord at 34" each. Knot both pieces together about 14" from one end. Make a second knot 4½" from the last knot made. (This will form the opening through which the mouth of the jar will go.)

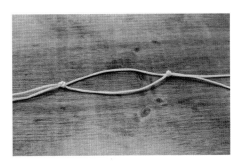

3. Take one loose strand from each knot and knot them together about 3" up from the last knots.

4. Repeat the last step for the other two loose strands. Then, repeat the last two steps one more time. When complete, there should be six knots in all. Slip the Mason jar, bottom up, into the holder just made.

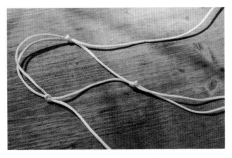

5. Cut off the stem of the silk flower very close to its base. Glue the flower onto the bottom of the Mason jar, taping it firmly down with painter's tape until the glue cures. Finally, knot the ends of the nylon to hang the feeder.

MAKING THE NECTAR

Add 4 parts water to 1 part granulated sugar. Boil the mixture at medium-high heat on a stovetop until the sugar is dissolved. When cool, add the nectar to your feeder and hang it in a sunny location.

Glass-Bottom Squirrel Feeder

"**S**quirrel!" It's an exclamation that can be heard all across the country. Especially in city parks. So where *did* all those squirrels come from? We can thank our nineteenth-century counterparts for that. Before then, squirrels were primarily a woodland creature. If you saw one in the city, it was most likely someone's pet. Then, in 1847, the city of Philadelphia released three squirrels in Franklin Square—much to the delight of the people who visited it. Towns across the country followed suit, and that's when the squirrel takeover began.

So why feed them? Because watching squirrels munch on peanuts is entertaining.

Supplies

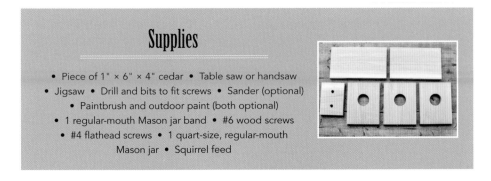

- Piece of 1" × 6" × 4' cedar • Table saw or handsaw
- Jigsaw • Drill and bits to fit screws • Sander (optional)
- Paintbrush and outdoor paint (both optional)
- 1 regular-mouth Mason jar band • #6 wood screws
- #4 flathead screws • 1 quart-size, regular-mouth Mason jar • Squirrel feed

MAKING YOUR SQUIRREL FEEDER

1. Using a table saw or handsaw, cut the board into the following dimensions:
- three pieces at 7" long (sides and front)
- one piece at 10" long (top)
- one piece at 9" long (back)
- one piece at 4" long (bottom)

2. Using the jigsaw, cut a 2" round hole in the front and side pieces. (The holes should be centered from side to side and their tops should be about 3" from the top of the board.) Then, drill two weep holes evenly spaced in the bottom piece.

3. With the table saw or a sander, bevel the back piece's top edge to an 8- to 10-degree angle. Drill and screw the top and back together. Paint the assembly, if desired, with outdoor paint.

4. Drill two holes at all the junction points of the wood pieces. Screw them together with the #6 wood screws.

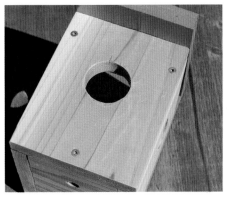

5. Center the Mason jar band over the front hole of the feeder and screw it into place with the small, #4 flathead screws.

6. Fill the jar with feed—peanuts in the shell seem much appreciated—and fit it onto the band. Attach the feeder onto a post or tree and wait to be entertained.

Gardener's
Gift Jar

Here's a secret about gift jars: although what's inside of them is important, it's really the presentation of the jar that sets it apart. Ribbon and calico are fine, but what better way to appeal to gardeners than to give them a bit of grass and a blossom? Call it green-thumb inspiration. Call it a cure for—or cause of—spring fever. Call it a fake flower and AstroTurf. Whichever you choose, this gift jar will be the start of a beautiful garden.

Supplies

- 1 quart-size, wide-mouth Mason jar lid and band
- One 4" × 4" piece of short-bladed synthetic turf
(Find it at your local big box hardware store; if you ask nicely, they may even give you a free sample.) • Utility scissors
- 1 small silk flower of the daisy variety • 1 small metal brad
- 1 quart-size, wide-mouth Mason jar

MAKING YOUR GIFT JAR

1. First, let's talk filler. Items that you might tuck inside your gift jar could include the following:
- Seed packets
- Plant stakes that correspond to the seeds
- Gardening twine or string
- A pair of gardening gloves
- Hand lotion

2. After you fill your jar, it's time to make the decorative lid. Simply use the jar lid as a template and cut out a circle of the synthetic turf. Pop the small silk flower off its faux stem, thread the brad through its center and attach the assembly to the turf. Sandwich the jar lid and the turf together and place it inside the band. Screw the band onto the jar, and you're done.

Jar Seed
Starters

1 n his seminal work, *On the Origin of Species*, Charles Darwin accredits James Beekman as the owner of the first greenhouse built in the United States. Constructed in 1764, it was situated on Beekman's Mount Pleasant estate in the countryside of Manhattan Island. Inside the greenhouse, visitors could find unfamiliar tropical specimens such as orange trees and oleander.

Although impossible to grow such plants to maturity inside a Mason jar, we can certainly start the *seeds* to such plants inside them. Plus, it's a great way to get a jump on the growing season.

Supplies

- Seed-starting soil, also known as germinating mix
- 4" peat pots, one for each bucket or pot (these aren't necessary, but they are encouraged, as they make transplanting later much easier) • Seeds • Plant sprayer • Small buckets or pots that measure approximately 4" wide at the top
- 1 short, wide-mouth Mason jar (a 16-ounce wide-mouth pint jar was used in this project)

MAKING YOUR SEED STARTERS

1. Loosely add geminating mix to peat pots and sow the seeds as recommended on the seed packets. Spray the newly planted seeds with water until saturated.

2. Slip the peat pots into the buckets or pots, and top with an inverted jar. Place the mini greenhouses in a sunny location indoors.

3. A convenient thing about using jars to germinate seeds is they form a perfect enclosure that keeps the seeds and seedlings well hydrated. So well hydrated, in fact, you might not have to spray the seeds with water until you remove the jars.

4. Thin the sprouts according to the recommendations on the seed packets. When mature enough to be on their own, and if the growing season permits, plant the seedlings and their peat pots directly into the ground.

Jar Band
Wind Chime

While people were still opening cans with hammers and chisels (no joke), entrepreneurs in the glass industry were busy applying for fruit jar closure patents. New inventions promised better, more hermetic seals, but most came and went. It wasn't until Alexander Hewitt Kerr brought the two-part metal disk and screw band to fame in 1912 that the Mason jar finally met its closure soulmate. The lid and band combination was dubbed "self-sealing," and it fit any Mason jar that had a smooth, machine-made lip. More than 100 years later, Kerr's two-part closures top almost all canning jars sold today.

Supplies

- Drill and small bit or tin punch with a die of ³⁄₃₂" or less • 12 regular-mouth jar bands
- Scissors • Approximately 6' of .018" bright beading wire • Approximately 45 silver tube-type #2 crimp beads • 12+ large acrylic crystal beads • Flat-nosed pliers
- 1 wide-mouth jar band

MAKING YOUR WIND CHIME

1. First, punch or drill two small holes in the sides of the 12 regular bands directly across from each other.

2. Cut an 18" piece of beading wire. Crimp on a bead at one end of the wire.

3. Thread the wire through one of the two holes in one of the bands. Slip on a crimp bead and a crystal bead. Gauge where the bead will fall in the center of the band. Once you have the larger bead centered, crimp the crimp bead flat with the flat-nosed pliers. Thread on another crimp bead, and flatten it right next to the crystal bead.

4. Thread the wire though the opposite hole in the band. Then, thread another crimp bead onto the wire. Hold the crimp bead about ½" away from the top hole of the jar band below, and crimp the bead flat.

5. Repeat Steps 3 and 4 until you have four bands and four crystal beads on the wire.

6. Repeat Steps 2 through 5 until you have three strands of four bands and four crystal beads.

7. Moving on to the larger jar band, drill three evenly spaced holes around its sides.

8. Slip the top of one of the band strand wires through one of the holes in the larger band. Place a crimp bead on the wire and crimp it so that the top of the small band hangs 3" to 4" down from the larger band.

9. Repeat this step for the other two strands of bands. Clip off the excess wire.

10. Finally, to make a hanger, drill or punch two small holes directly opposite each other on the top of the larger jar band. Slip an 18" to 20" piece of wire into the holes, crimping a bead on the wire's ends.

11. Find the center of the wire, and fold it in half. Slip a crimp bead onto the folded wire and slide it downward, positioning it in the center of the larger band. Crimp the bead flat.

Mason Jar
Bell

When I first started constructing a bell using a Mason jar, I had no idea what sound it would make. Would the wood clapper I chose cause it to "thud" or "clink"? To my pleasant surprise, it does neither. The wooden clapper makes a delicate "gong" sound when it strikes the glass.

Although Mason jar bells can handle a light breeze, it is best to hang them in protected spots if putting them outdoors. On a porch or under an eave to protect them from harsh winds is ideal. Indoors, any place that catches a breeze and a ray of light will make the jar sing.

Supplies

• 1 quart-size, regular-mouth Mason jar • Bottle cutter and finishing equipment • Drill and small bit or metal punch • 1 regular-size jar lid and band or a regular-size reproduction jar lid • Craft glue, such as E6000 • Needle-nose pliers • 12" of #16 chain • 2 small eye screws • ¾" wooden ball (found at a craft store) • 1 salvaged fork • Tin snips

MAKING YOUR BELL

1. Cut approximately 1" off the bottom of the jar and finish the cut edge according to the technical instructions in this book (p. 35–36) or according to the bottle cutter's instructions.

2. Drill or punch a small hole in the center of the lid. Glue the washer to the inside of the lid, aligning holes in lid and washer. Using needle-nose pliers, unlink the chain in three sections of 5", 7", and one section of one link only. Feed the opened link of the 7" length through the *top* of the hole in the lid and reattach the 5" length to it. (The shorter chain length will be hanging inside the jar.)

3. Next, again using the pliers, insert the 2 small eye screws into the wooden ball so that they are directly opposite each other.

4. Attach the last link in the 5" chain to one of the eye screws in the wooden ball. Into the eye screw on the opposite side of the ball, attach the single link of chain.

5. Take the salvaged fork and cut its handle off with the tin snips. Drill a small hole at the top of the fork, and curl the tines with the needle-nose pliers.

6. Attach the fork to the single link at the bottom of the wooden ball.

7. Slip the entire chain, ball, and fork assembly through the Mason jar and twist on the lid. Ding, dong, done.

Tabletop Mason Jar
Water Fountain

N ew York City lays claim to the oldest decorative water fountain in the United States. Constructed in 1842 in celebration of the completion of the Croton Aqueduct, the Croton Fountain shot 50 feet into the air, amazing its onlookers.

This Mason jar water fountain doesn't reach those heights, but it's incredibly easy to make and is amazing in its own little way. Plus, it's small enough to set on a table, so it has that going for it too.

Supplies

- 1 quart-size Mason jar (either regular- or wide-mouth will do)
- Bottle cutter and finishing equipment • Small, submersible water fountain pump • Decorative stones—medium to small size • Clear tubing to fit pump's discharge outlet, if necessary • 1 Mason jar lid and band to fit jar used, or a one-piece vintage lid • Water
- Medium-size waterproof vessel

MAKING YOUR FOUNTAIN

1. Cut approximately 1" off the bottom of the jar and finish the cut edge according to the technical instructions in this book (p. 35–36) or according to the bottle cutter's instructions.

2. Nestle the pump at the center of the vessel and add medium-sized stones around the pump to keep it centered.

3. Connect a small length of tubing to the pump if you wish or if you need to lengthen the pump's discharge outlet to bypass the stones. Fill the vessel with remaining stones of the smaller variety. (By finishing with a layer of smaller stones, the jar will stay level.)

4. Put the lid on the jar and place it over the pump.

5. Fill the vessel with water just shy of the bottle's bottom rim. (If the water is above the rim, the pump will most likely create a vacuum, causing water to be drawn up into the jar.) Plug the fountain in an electrical outlet and unplug to the sound of bubbling water.

Malted Milk Ball
Cocoa

While on a trip to Paris in 1785, Thomas Jefferson wrote in a letter to his friend John Adams, "The superiority of [hot] chocolate, both for health and nourishment, will soon give it the preference over tea and coffee in America . . ." As evidenced by a coffeehouse on just about every twenty-first-century-America street corner, Jefferson missed the mark on that prediction. But as for his "superiority of chocolate" proclamation, I couldn't agree more.

So, to pay homage to Mr. Jefferson, here's a tasty malted milk ball version of the drink. The mix is a perfect occupant of another slice of history, a Mason jar—preferably Ball, or its title doesn't work as well.

Supplies

- Large mixing bowl and spoon • ¾ cup granulated sugar
- ¾ cup unsweetened cocoa powder • 1½ cups malted milk powder
- ¾ cup nondairy creamer • ¼ teaspoon fine ground sea salt
- Canning funnel (optional, but very handy)
- 1 one-quart Ball Mason jar • 1 band and lid to fit the Mason jar used

MAKING YOUR COCOA

1. Mix the dry ingredients together.

2. Add them to the jar using the canning funnel. Screw on the two-part cap to store.

3. To serve: Mix 2 rounded tablespoons into an 8-ounce cup of hot milk. In lieu of standard marshmallows, toss in a few malted milk balls.

Dark Forest Trail Mix

Pemmican—trail mix's precursor—consisted of dried buffalo, moose, or caribou, and it was traditionally mixed with animal fat and berries. Not only was it a high-energy snack, but it lasted for months. Somewhere along the road to the twentieth century, someone ditched the dried meat and added peanuts, and vegetarians everywhere rejoiced. Although surfers claim they invented the new combo in 1968, 10 years earlier, Jack Kerouac's *The Dharma Bums* prepared a "big bag of peanuts and raisins" for energy food. Of course, one could argue that was gorp, but we're not here to argue.

Supplies

- 2 cups roasted sea salted almonds • 1 cup raw whole cashews
- 1 cup chocolate yogurt-coated raisins • 1 cup dried cherries
- 1 cup unsweetened flaked coconut • Large mixing bowl and spoon
- 1 quart-size and 1 pint-size Mason jar or 3 pint-size jars
- Lids and bands to fit the jars

MAKING YOUR TRAIL MIX

1. Measure the ingredients.

2. Mix the ingredients in a large bowl. Transfer the mix to the jars to store.

3. Or just start snarfing it right out of the bowl.

Pineapple-Infused Vodka

he partnership of Mason jars and white lightening didn't end with the repeal of prohibition. Even today, some purveyors of spirits choose to bottle their wares in the humble vessels. These traditionalists pass along a bit of American history as one might pass a jar of hooch among a group of friends. By the end of the night, the communal cup will be empty, and everyone will be sporting a dent in the bridge of their nose where the jar bumped them as they took a long pull, just like those imbibers of decades past.

In honor of moonshiners of old and new, here's a less volatile preparation that doesn't require a still: pineapple-infused vodka. Complete the concoction with a Mason jar cocktail glass and a summery drink recipe using your homemade hooch, and you'll be good to go.

Supplies

- 1 fresh pineapple, clean, peeled, and cubed
- 1 quart-size Mason jar • 1 band and lid to fit the quart-sized Mason jar used • 1 bottle of unflavored vodka
- Craft glue, such as E6000 • 1 glass candlestick, about 4" high (a great place to find these is in secondhand shops)
- One 8-ounce, wide-mouth Collection Elite half-pint Ball jar
- Orange soda • Maraschino cherries, minced

MAKING YOUR INFUSED VODKA

1. Place the cubed pineapple pieces into the Mason jar and cover with vodka.

2. Put it in a cool, dark place for a week or two to infuse.

MAKING YOUR MASON JAR COCKTAIL GLASS

1. Apply glue to the top of the candlestick and center the bottom of the half-pint jar over it.

2. Let the glue cure as stipulated by the adhesive's directions.

MAKING YOUR VODKA FRUIT CRUSH COCKTAIL

1. Mix 6 ounces orange soda with one shot of pineapple-infused vodka.

2. Add to liquid two minced maraschino cherries and two pieces infused pineapple.

3. Enjoy on a hot day—preferably poolside.

Vanilla-Infused Sugar

*W*hen the United States entered World War II and supply chains were broken, home bakers were left in a culinary quandary. In an effort to ease their dismay, "sugarless" recipes for sweets sprung up everywhere in the form of recipe books and pamphlets. In them, honey, maple syrup, and corn syrup were deemed acceptable substitutes for their precious baking staple. But if you're going to infuse sugar with vanilla, there is no substitute for either. Sparkling, crystalline sugar plus Madagascar vanilla beans make a delicious duo that would have popped Rosie's rivets.

Supplies

- 1 fresh Madagascar vanilla bean (not inexpensive, but worth every penny) • Sharp knife and cutting board • 2 soup spoons • 2 cups of organic white sugar • Mixing bowl • Canning funnel (not necessary, but helpful) • One 1-pint Mason jar • 1 band and lid to fit the Mason jar used

MAKING YOUR SUGAR

1. Using the knife and cutting board, slice the vanilla bean open the long way. Holding one end of the bean with a spoon, use the other spoon to scrape the seeds from the bean.

2. Put the sugar into a bowl and add the seeds to it. Use the back of a spoon to push/incorporate the seeds into the sugar.

3. Funnel the sugar into the Mason jar. Screw on the cap and leave for a week or more to infuse the flavors. Use the concoction like regular sugar—in coffee, sprinkled on oatmeal . . . you get the idea.

Orange and Clove Room Scent Shaker

We can thank the military and insects for modern-day air fresheners, as they were born out of the pressurized insecticide sprays developed to protect soldiers from bug bites. In 1948, the technology jumped in from the outdoors, giving us homes smelling of, ironically, stuff found outdoors. A scent-cloud of imitation pine, the freshener bathed everyone and everything in its wake.

On the other hand, a jar room scent shaker, filled with whole spices and essential oils, fills a room with a light, natural scent. And because a shaker lets the air do all the work, it puts just the right amount of scent right where you need it.

Supplies

• 1 regular-size jar band and lid • Metal window screen, about 4" square per jar • Scissors • Whole spices and essential oil (cloves and sweet orange were used in this project) • 1 small, regular-mouth Mason jar (a 4-ounce quilted crystal jelly jar was used for this project) • 1 inexpensive bracelet (optional, but fun)

MAKING YOUR SHAKER

1. Use the jar lid as a template to cut a circle out of the metal screen. Slip the screen into the jar band as you would a jar lid and set aside.

2. Mix 2 or more tablespoons of whole cloves with 20 to 40 drops of sweet orange oil. Place into jar and top with the screened band.

3. Decorate the band with an inexpensive bracelet to add a little personality. To release the scent, give the jar a shake whenever the room needs refreshing.

Homemade Butter in a Jar

he first factory in the United States dedicated exclusively to making butter was established in 1856 in Orange County, New York. It was owned by one R. W. Woodhull, and the butter maker's name was George George. (So nice, he was named twice.) Before then, butter churning was, primarily, a home-based enterprise. Although centuries have passed, the technique for making butter has changed little: put heavy cream in a container of some sort and whip the daylights out of it.

There's science behind turning cream into butter that involves disrupting the position of fat molecules, or something like that. But to the uninitiated, turning cream into butter seems like magic.

Supplies

- 1 quart-size Mason jar, chilled
- 1 band and lid to fit the Mason jar used
- Strainer • Cool water
- Large spoon • Plastic wrap
- Heavy whipping cream

MAKING BUTTER MAGIC

1. Pour the cold whipping cream into the jar, put on the lid and band, and shake. And shake and shake some more. After 10 minutes, the cream will have expanded, and you will have made whipped cream. But that's no time to stop.

2. Keep shaking! At 20 minutes, the whipped cream will start to compact and make butter, separating it from the butter's milk. Yes, you've made buttermilk too.

3. Strain the butter, but make sure to save the buttermilk to drink or use for cooking later. Rinse the clumps of butter with cool water.

4. Knead the butter with the back of the spoon to force out more buttermilk; this will help keep the butter from souring too quickly. Rinse some more, knead some more, and then rinse one final time.

5. Put the clumps onto plastic wrap and shape them into a ball of buttery goodness.

Fruit Smoothie
in a Jar

I t wasn't as if people weren't pureeing fruit before 1937 when Fred Osius debuted his Waring blender to the world. They were. They just weren't calling them "smoothies" then. It wasn't until Waring came out with their blender's companion cookbook from 1940, that similar drinks were referred to as "children's milk smoothees." Although the name was there, the contents weren't. Those early concoctions didn't contain ice, but they did call for ingredients such as tomatoes, yellow turnips, and raw liver.

I'd like to think Mr. Osius foresaw the popularity of today's versions of smoothies and Mason jars converging. That's because a Mason jar with a regular mouth can be substituted for a blender's pitcher. You know what that means: we can blend and serve individual smoothies in Mason jars. And that, my fellow smoothie lovers, is a multitasking miracle if ever there was one.

Supplies

- A pint-size, regular-mouth Mason jar (one per person)
- Your favorite smoothie ingredients, which will include ¼ cup liquid, ¾ cup ice, and 1 cup fruit
- Blender

MAKING YOUR FRUIT SMOOTHIE

1. In order, add to the Mason jar the liquid, then the ice, and finally the fruit. Twist on the blender's blade and gasket assembly. Insert the inverted jar into the blender.

2. Blend at a low speed and gradually increase the speed to high when the fruit starts to migrate toward the bottom of the jar.

3. When all the ice has turned to slush, you know your smoothie is ready to enjoy. But be warned—a tasty smoothie can result in brain freeze, so sip responsibly.

Night-Before Granola & Yogurt Breakfast Sundaes

I n 1894, Dr. Connor Harold Lacey of Toledo, Ohio, first coined the word "granola." His recipe included graham flour, not rolled oats. It wasn't until the 1940s that nutrition pioneer Adelle Davis jettisoned the graham and created the grandfather of contemporary granola. Popularity of the crunchy stuff took off with the hippie movement of the 1960s. Nowadays, hippies might be in short supply, but granola is not.

Granola by itself is tasty; layering it with yogurt and fruit is delicious. Serving it as a sundae is a morning decadence that will empress even the finickiest of palates.

Supplies

- One 8-ounce, wide-mouth half-pint Mason jar, one per person
- Yogurt (French vanilla is always a good choice)
- Fresh fruit

MAKING YOUR SUNDAES

1. Place ⅓ cup of granola into each Mason jar.

2. Top with ⅓ cup yogurt. Finish off with a layer of fruit, sliced or otherwise. (Getting fancy with fruit presentation will earn you extra points.)

3. After sealing the individual jars, pop them in the refrigerator to rest overnight and infuse their flavors.

Salad & Dressing
To-Go Jar

We've already learned the secret of a regular-mouth Mason jar fitting a standard blender assembly, but wide-mouth jars have a secret that'll blow your mind too. It's this: individual applesauce and gelatin containers fit inside them. That means we can put stuff inside a jar—say, a salad—and add a dressing to the applesauce or gelatin container and turn it into a to-go jar perfect for a healthy and easy weekday lunch.

Supplies

- 1 wide-mouth Mason jar (a quart-sized jar was used for this project)
- Salad fixings and dressing
- 1 leftover plastic applesauce or gelatin container
- 1 wide-mouth jar lid and band

MAKING YOUR TO-GO SALAD

1. After cleaning my salad fixings, I like to layer the ingredients inside the jar. Although completely unnecessary, it does look pretty.

2. Leave the last 2" or so of the jar empty to make room for the applesauce/gelatin container, which you'll fill with your favorite dressing.

3. Then, pop the container of dressing inside the mouth of the Mason jar, securing it in place with the jar lid and band.

4. When it comes time for lunch, simply empty the sauce into the jar, put the lid and band back onto the jar, and give it a good shake to distribute the dressing.

Jar Band
Trivet

The earliest trivets made for kitchen use were fabricated by blacksmiths, and they sported feet that raised pots over hot coals. Their contemporary counterparts have the much less taxing job of keeping countertops and tables from getting burnt or scratched. Go into any kitchen accessories store and you'll see trivets made of tile, fabric, and wood. But you probably won't see one made of Mason jar bands.

Coupling wide- and regular-mouth bands together and wrapping them in novelty yarn transforms the humble Mason jar closures into an unexpected shape. Tying the shapes together to form a trivet is something fresh and new.

Supplies

- 3 wide-mouth Mason jar bands
- 3 regular-mouth Mason jar bands
- Novelty yarn • Scissors
- Darning needle

MAKING YOUR TRIVET

1. Nestle a small band inside a larger one. Start wrapping the two bands together with the novelty yarn, making sure the bands are completely hidden as you wrap.

2. When finished wrapping, cut the yarn and use a darning needle to weave in the ends. Repeat this process for the other four bands.

3. When all three sets of bands have been completed, use a length of yarn and the darning needle to stitch the yarn-wrapped bands together. (Just a few stitches will suffice.)

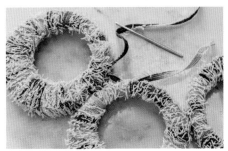

4. Bring the yarn ends to the back/underside of the trivet and knot securely. Trim the yarn close to the knot.

Jar Tissue
Pop-Up

Much like room air fresheners, the needs of soldiers on the battlefield can be credited for the inception of disposable tissues. In 1914, cotton was in short supply. Paper product manufacturer Kimberly-Clark started producing Cellucotton as a substitute. First used as bandages in World War I, Cellucotton led to the creation of Kleenex. Around that time, a Chicago inventor came up with an idea that allowed for tissues to "pop up" from a box. Kimberly-Clark decided to package Kleenexes in the boxes and nose-blowing history was born.

The magic in the pop-up box isn't in the box itself; it's in the way the tissues are folded inside the box that makes them magically pop up. Knowing this tidbit is the secret behind making a Jar Tissue Pop-Up.

Supplies

- One half-gallon, wide-mouth Mason jar
- Isopropyl alcohol • Glass paint (the color "sea glass" was used in this project) • Small painting sponge
- 1 emery board • 1 square box of tissues
- 1 wide-mouth jar band

MAKING YOUR TISSUE POP-UP

1. Wash and dry the jar and then wipe it down with isopropyl alcohol.

2. Using the paint sponge, sponge the glass paint over the entire outside of the jar.

3. When the paint has cured, use an emery board to carefully sand off the paint from the jar's embossing.

4. Open the box of tissues at one end.

5. Remove the tissues from the box, keeping them in one stack.

6. Free the corner of the tissue on the top of the pile, and gently feed approximately half of the pile into the top of the jar, short side of tissues down.

7. Screw on the jar's band and you're done.

Bathroom Set & Granite Tray

Pump bottles filled with liquid hand soap might seem like they've been around forever, but it wasn't until 1980 when entrepreneur Robert R. Taylor decided there had to be a better, less messy alternative to bar soap when washing up at the sink. Knowing that putting liquid soap in a pump bottle was not a patentable innovation, Mr. Taylor thought the best means of avoiding competition would be to corner the market on bottle hand pumps. Only two manufacturers in the United States were making them at the time, so Mr. Taylor placed an order for 100 million of them, creating a backlog of two years and thereby solidifying his soap-in-a-pump idea.

Turning a Mason jar into a soap pump might not be a patentable innovation either. When clever crafters started doing it, manufacturers jumped on the bandwagon, producing made-to-fit Mason jar lids with integrated pumps. Either way—using store-bought lids or doing it yourself—Mason jar soap and lotion pumps are elevated from lowly containers to royal status, thanks to a fabricated granite tray.

Supplies

- One 12" × 12" × ⅜" square piece of granite • A wet saw (Don't have a wet saw? Use ⅜"-thick wood material instead of the granite.) • Clear silicone caulk • 2 empty plastic bottles with pumps • Hacksaw • Utility knife • 2 sets of regular-mouth jar lids and bands • Felt-tip pen • Metal hole punch or drill and small bit • Small, sharp utility scissors • 2 pint-size, regular-mouth Mason jars

MAKING YOUR BATHROOM SET

1. First, to fabricate the granite tray, use the wet saw to cut the granite into the following rectangles:
- one piece at 3½" × 6⅝" (for the bottom)
- two pieces at 1" × 6⅝" (for the sides)
- two pieces at 1" × 3½" (for the ends)

2. Glue all the adjacent edges together using clear silicone caulk. When joints are dry, run a small bead of caulk on the inside seams to seal.

3. To make the soap pumps, use a hacksaw to cut off the threaded necks of the plastic pump bottles. Deburr the edges of the cut plastic with a utility knife blade, if necessary.

4. Using the plastic necks as a template, mark a circle in the center of each jar lid with a felt-tip pen. Punch or drill a hole in the center of the mark to allow access for your scissor blade. With the scissors, widen the hole to the marked circumference.

5. Using silicone, glue the threaded piece into the hole from the underside of the lid and let it dry completely. Run a small bead of silicone on the upper part of the lid next to the threads there as well. Let dry. Screw the pumping mechanisms onto the jars and place in the granite tray.

Swizzle Stick
Pop-Up Holder

How does one fish the olive out of his martini without getting his fingers wet? That was the question amateur inventor Jay Sindler asked himself in 1937 as he sat in the bar of Boston's Ritz-Carlton Hotel. Before then, tipplers had to use their digits to nab the little guys. Mr. Sindler, who was struck by inspiration, brought us out of the dark ages and invented the swizzle stick. His original idea was for a small wooden spear onto which the non-olive end could be emblazoned with a drinking establishment's name or logo. Then World War II and our grand adventure of visiting the moon spurred the plastic and injection molding business. It was then, much like Apollo 11, that swizzle stick production took off.

Although swizzle sticks and drink stirrers have different jobs these days, the latter are oftentimes still referred to as the former. Which is why this is a swizzle stick pop-up holder and not a drink stirrer pop-up holder. Plus, swizzle is much more fun to say.

Supplies

- Drill and bit or metal hole punch to fit ⁸/₃₂" rod • 1 regular-mouth lid and band • 1 wide-mouth lid and band • Nontoxic glue
- 1' length of ⁸/₃₂" threaded rod • 1 wide-mouth 1½ pint or quart-size Mason jar • Hacksaw • 3 nylon locking nuts to fit rod
- 1 acorn nut to fit rod end • Swizzle sticks

MAKING YOUR SWIZZLE STICK POP-UP

1. Drill or punch a hole in the center of *both* lids, slightly larger than the threaded rod. Glue each band to the corresponding ring.

2. Measure the threaded rod by inserting it into the jar and adding on about ½". Cut to length with a hacksaw.

3. At one end of the rod, screw on one nylon locking nut, about ½" from the end of the rod. Then slip on the smallest lid/band assembly and follow up with a second nylon locking nut. It's best if the lid assembly spins freely between the nuts.

4. Repeat the last step for the other end of the rod, slipping on the larger lid/band assembly and following up with the acorn nut. Again, it's best if the lid assembly spins freely between the nylon nut and acorn nut.

5. Fill the lower lid with swizzle sticks and pop the rod contraption inside the jar. When the jar is opened and the lid lifted, the swizzle sticks will rise and lean outward for easy picking.

INSPIRED STORAGE

Triptych Twine Station

Whether used indoors or out, a twine station keeps everything in easy reach. And because the spools are kept under glass, they stay clean and secure. No rolling across the floor for these guys, only to have the cat or dog get the wrong impression.

I've chosen to do a twine triptych of sorts, but one larger spool of twine—using a pint-size Mason jar—would work perfectly as well.

Supplies

- Scrap piece of ½" plywood (birch was used in this project)
- Table saw or handsaw • Six #4 × ⅜" long wood screws
- Drill and bits to fit screws • Metal punch, optional
- 3 wide-mouth bands and lids • 3 balls of colorful twine, approximately 2" in diameter • 3 wide-mouth, half-pint Mason jars • Wood glue • 180-grit sandpaper

MAKING YOUR TWINE STATION

1. Using a table saw or handsaw, cut the plywood into the following sizes:
- one piece at 10" × 13" for the back
- one piece at 4" × 13" for the shelf

2. With the #6 wood screws and the wood glue, glue and screw the smaller board (the shelf) to the larger board 3½" from the lower edge of the larger board (the back).

3. When the glue is dry, lightly sand the assembly as needed with 180-grit sandpaper.

4. Punch or drill a ¼" hole in the center of each of the three lids. Punch or drill two smaller holes on either side of the center hole. Center the lid assemblies down the length of the shelf, and screw them into place through the holes, using the #4 screws.

5. Drill through the ¼" holes in the lids and through the wood below.

6. Pop the twine into the jars and feed one end of the twine through the hole in the lid and shelf, letting the twine dangle. For the full twine station effect, hang it on some pegboard along with your other gardening or crafting tools.

Fire Starters & Matches Jar

There's nothing more delightful than spending a crisp evening in front of a fire. Whether it's indoors by a fireplace or outdoors at a fire ring, accumulating the wood is the hardest part. The easiest part is getting the fire started, thanks to salvaged wood shavings and old candles. That's because when you combine them, they make great fire starters. Couple them with long matches and pop them into a 1-gallon collector's Ball jar, and they are pretty enough to display or give as a gift.

Supplies

• 1 cookie sheet • Aluminum foil • Small wax-paper nut/party cup (the individual cups from cardboard egg cartons work too) • Wood shavings leftover from a past project (natural wood only— no treated wood!) • 1 old saucepan • Old candles • 13"-long matches • One 1-gallon collector's Ball jar with decorative lid • Craft glue

MAKING YOUR FIRE STARTER & MATCHES JAR

1. Line the cookie sheet with aluminum foil. Lay the party cups on the foil, right-side up. Pack each cup with wood shavings.

2. Melt old candles over low heat. Slowly pour the wax into each cup until full.

3. Put the matches into the jar and glue the matchbox's striking surface to the inside of the jar's lid. When the wax has cooled and hardened, fill the other side of the jar with the fire starters.

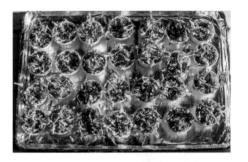

Keep It Sharp
Pencil Keeper

Pencils were first whittled to a point by knives. Then, in 1828, Frenchman Bernard Lassimone applied for a patent for the first pencil sharpener, which took about as much work as the whittling route. Not surprisingly, it didn't catch on. It wasn't until 10 years later that fellow Frenchman Therry des Estwaux devised the prism sharpener, the forerunner for pocket sharpeners we have today. Even though advancements in pencil sharpeners continued—from "crank" types to electric—prism sharpeners are as popular as ever. They're also the reason why this project does double duty, since it stores pencils as well as sharpens them.

Supplies

• Drill • Bit or metal hole punch to fit hole in sharpener
• Small bit to fit 4-40 × ⅜" pan-head screws • 1 lid and band to fit jar
• 1 two-part prism-type pencil sharpener with integrated shavings catcher
• 2 small screws (4-40 × ⅜" long pan-head machine screws were used in this project) • 2 small washers to fit screws • 2 small nuts to fit screws
• 1 half-gallon, wide-mouth Mason jar

MAKING YOUR PENCIL KEEPER

1. Punch or drill a hole in the center of the lid the same size as the pencil sharpener's opening.

2. Drill two small holes on either side of the pencil sharpener hole to fit the pan-head screws. Drill two corresponding holes in the top piece of the pencil sharpener.

3. Using the screws, washers, and nuts, attach the sharpener's top piece to the underside of the jar's lid.

4. Fit the shavings catcher on the underside of the sharpener's top piece.

5. Pop pencils inside the jar and screw on the pencil sharpener assembly. Note: as the pencils get shorter, you can downsize the jar to a quart size.

Entryway Catch-All

Party 7:30 pm
Wednesday
Lake Anne Park!

Things to buy:
eggs
milk
bread
dark chocolate

artin Cooper, an engineer at Motorola, made the first cell phone call on the streets of New York City on April 3, 1973. The "portable" device weighed in at a hefty 2.2 pounds and was the size of a lunchbox. Lucky for us, cell phones have shrunk to a diminutive size; unluckily, we've been misplacing them ever since.

Cell phones, along with keys and billfolds, are the holy trinity of pocket accoutrements. So important yet so easily lost, everyone should have a catch-all to corral them. And this project is up to the task.

Supplies

- One piece of 2' × 2' ½" × ¾" pine board • Table saw or handsaw • Sandpaper, 120- or 180-grit • Pencil
- 1 wide-mouth Mason jar band • Jigsaw • Drill
- Center punch • Two #4 × ½" flathead wood screws
- Wood glue • Two #6 wood screws • 180-grit sandpaper
- Paint brush, primer, and paint • One piece of 11" × 14" corkboard • Sticky-back foam tape, optional
- One decorative hook • One 16-ounce wide-mouth pint Collection Elite Ball Mason jar, which is approximately 3½" tall x 3½" wide.

MAKING YOUR CATCH-ALL

1. Using a table saw or handsaw, cut the board into one piece measuring 1' × 2' (for the back) and another piece measuring 1' × 5" (for the shelf). Sand both pieces.

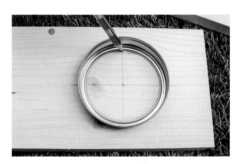

2. With a pencil and using the inside dimension of the jar band as a template, mark a circle on the shelf, centering the band from front to back and approximately 2" from one edge.

3. Cut out the circle with a jigsaw. Sand the inside of the hole.

4. Punch or drill two small holes at the top lip of the band directly opposite from each other. Use a center punch to chamfer the holes. Attach the band over the hole using the #4 screws.

5. Attach the shelf piece to the back with wood glue and the #6 screws so the top of the shelf is 6" up from the bottom of the back.

6. Sand and paint the shelving assembly.

7. Apply the corkboard with sticky-back foam tape (or wood glue) to the back piece of the shelf, ½" down and centered side to side.

8. Center and attach the decorative hook. Screw the Mason jar into its band.

Wine-Not Desk Organizer

Mason jars have something in common with wine bottles: their approximate diameter. Wine comes in as many varieties as the vessels in which they're bottled. They start out at 2⅜" and expand to 3⅜" for large pinots. Those who manufacture wine racks must keep these measurements in mind, which brings us back to Mason jars. Quart-size jars measure approximately 3½" and fall right into the wine bottle sizing sweet spot. Swap out wine bottles for Mason jars and you have an instant desk organizer.

Supplies

- A thrifted wine bottle rack in an appropriate size for your desk organization needs. (When shopping for wine racks to use, you will want to fit a Mason jar into them before you make any commitments, as some wine racks provide a more secure fit than others.)
- You'll also need as many Mason jars as there are slots in your wine rack. (Wide-mouth jars were used in this project as they're easier to reach into.)

MAKING YOUR DESK ORGANIZER

1. Insert the Mason jars into the wine rack.

2. Make sure to rest the necks of the jars on the rack's frame.

Outdoor Wooden
Dining Caddy

ome of my favorite woodworking projects are those that use leftover wood from other projects. This is one of them. What the former project was, I can't remember. All I know is there was a piece of stock in the leftover bin that spoke to me. It said, "Pick me!" I asked, "What for?" It replied, "To make an outdoor wooden dining caddy, you idiot." Why it insulted me, I have no idea. As to the dining caddy part, it was totally right.

Supplies

- One piece of ¼" × 4" × 4" wood, scrap or otherwise
- Table saw or handsaw • A drill and a 1¼" hole saw or a jigsaw
- A hammer and finishing nails • Wood glue
- 3 pint-size, regular-mouth Mason jars • 180-grit sand paper
- Paint brush, primer, and paint (optional)

MAKING YOUR CADDY

1. Using a table saw or handsaw, cut your wood stock into the following dimensions:
- two pieces at 11" × 3½" (for the sides)
- two pieces at 3½" × 3½" (for the ends)
- one piece at 10" × 3½" (for the bottom)

2. Drill or jigsaw three 1¼" holes evenly spaced down the center of both side pieces, placing one on center at 5½" and the other two centered at 2½" and 8½", respectively.

3. Use wood glue and finishing nails to assemble all five pieces of the caddy.

4. Sand, prime, and paint the caddy, if desired.

5. Add the 3 pint-size jars to the caddy and fill with flatware.

Clip & Binder
Holder

paper clip is much like a Mason jar. Their shapes have changed very little since their inceptions. Take a look at William Middlebrook's 1899 patent drawing for the machinery that would eventually make the Gem clip, and you'll see what I mean. Although Middlebrook had dozens of competitors, like the 1903 Banjo paper clip which looks kind of like a banjo, and the 1899 Daisy Clip, which looks nothing like a daisy. Both were decorative to be sure, but it was the Gem design that became our go-to clip.

We give paper clips little thought, until we can't find one, that is. With this clip and binder holder, those little humble masterpieces will always be on display and within easy reach.

Supplies

- Craft glue, such as E6000 • One half-pint, regular-mouth Mason jar • One regular-mouth jar band and lid
- One 1½" to 2" round magnet (a 16-pound pull magnet was used in this project)

MAKING YOUR HOLDER

1. Glue the jar and band together using the craft glue. When cured, plop the magnet on the underside of the lid.

2. Fill the jar with binders, throw some clips on the magnetized lid, and screw it on the jar.

Lion's Paw
Accent Lamp

onsidering there are approximately 620,000 kilometers of oceanic coastline on earth, you'd think lion's paw seashells would be easy to find. They're not. Sure, after a storm one might wash up here and there, but, primarily, these big, beautiful shells make their way onto dry land via shrimping boat dredges. Whether you find one the old-fashioned way by combing the beach or in an aisle of your favorite craft store, lion's paws make perfect accent lampshades as the light source illuminates the area while it highlights the shell itself.

Supplies

- Drill and bits to accommodate lamp works • Small block of wood, approximately 1½" square • Lamp repair cord with integrated plug • 1 one-piece, regular-mouth reproduction Mason jar lid • ½" length of standard threaded lamp nipple and nut to fit • 1 keyless light bulb socket with a candelabra base and cover • 1 large lion's paw seashell, or any large scallop shell • Pencil • Small scrap of ¼" plywood • Scissors • 1 pint-size, regular-mouth Mason jar • Vase filler, such as sand, pebbles, or sea glass • One 4- to 7-watt light bulb with a candelabra base or CFL equivalent • Small handsaw or jigsaw

MAKING YOUR LION'S PAW LAMP

1. Drill a hole in the center of the wooden block to fit the candelabra socket cover. Perpendicular to the hole, drill another smaller hole to fit the the lamp cord.

2. Drill a hole in the top of the Mason jar lid to accommodate the threaded lamp nipple.

3. Feed the lamp wire through the smaller hole in the side of the wooden block and up through the larger hole on top. Connect the wire to the candelabra socket according to the manufacturer's directions. Insert the lamp base into the larger hole of the wood block.

4. Slip the candelabra socket cover over the socket. Then, thread the lamp nipple into the lamp socket. Put a dab of caulk onto the top of the jar lid near the hole. (This will glue the block to the lid.) Then insert the pipe nipple into the hole and thread the nut onto the nipple and tighten.

5. Trace the lower part of the seashell onto the plywood. With a small handsaw, cut out the shape and glue it to the back side of the seashell with caulk.

6. When the caulk is completely dry, glue the seashell assembly to the block of wood opposite from the cord side with additional caulk. Let dry.

7. Fill the Mason jar with the vase filler. Screw the bulb into the socket and turn on the lamp.

Outdoor Solar Wall Sconces

he first photovoltaic module, identified as a solar battery at the time, was built in 1954 by Bell Laboratories. Its prohibitive cost landed it in the curiosity column among the scientific set. Then, in the 1960s, the space program stepped in and took the technology to the heavens and back. Advancement and declining costs converged with the 1970s energy crisis and established photovoltaics as a viable energy source for non-space implementations. Jump ahead to 1978 and solar cells were in calculators, and then, just a few decades later, they started popping up in gardens everywhere as path lights. Quite the pedigree for something we can pick up for a couple of dollars at the hardware store.

Supplies

- 2 secondhand metal candle wall sconces (thrift stores are filled with them) • 180-grit sandpaper • Drill and small drill bit • Stainless steel appliance epoxy spray paint
- 2 solar garden stake lights (the underside of the top mechanism should be approximately the same diameter as the inside measurement of a regular-size jar band)
- Painter's tape • All-weather clear caulk • 2 regular-mouth Mason jar bands • 2 quart-size, regular-mouth Mason jars

MAKING YOUR SCONCES

1. Clean and sand the candle wall sconces, if necessary. Drill several small weep holes into the outer perimeter of the sconces past where the Mason jars will center. Spray the sconces with epoxy spray paint.

2. Unscrew the top of the garden lights. (Note the size of the inside diameter of the light versus the inside diameter of the jar band in the photo.)

3. Clean and sand the trim of the lights. Tape off the solar cell on top and shoot with paint.

4. When dry, use caulk to glue the solar light tops to the jar bands.

5. Glue the jars at the center of the sconce bases with the caulk, avoiding the weep holes, and let dry completely before exposing your new solar wall sconces to the elements.

Moonbeam
Stakes

Modern glow-in-the-dark paint must be exposed to a light source for it to glow, but back in the 1900s it was a different story. Found on everything from watch faces to airplane dials, early luminescent paints needed no light source to throw a glow, because they contained radium. They worked great, but they were also toxic. These moonbeam stakes, on the other hand, may look pernicious, but they are perfectly safe. They will, however, need a light charge to glow. But, hey—I'll take minor inconvenience over radioactivity any day.

Supplies

- Handsaw • 1" dowel, approximately 18" for every jar
- Drill and bit to accommodate screws • Mini Mason jars with coordinating lids (the jars used in this project measure 3¼" high and 2" in diameter) • Stainless steel appliance epoxy spray paint • Panhead wood screws, ¾" to 1" long, one for every jar • Safety swabs
- Glow-in-the-dark craft paint

MAKING YOUR MOONBEAM STAKES

1. Saw the dowel in 18" lengths and clip one end at an angle. In the other end, drill a pilot hole for the screws. Drill holes into the center of each of the jars' lids, and shoot the dowels with spray paint.

2. Attach a lid to the flat end of the dowel with a wood screw; repeat for each jar lid and dowel.

3. Wash and dry the Mason jars. With safety swabs, dab haphazard blobs of glow-in-the-dark paint on the inside of the jars.

4. When the paint is dry, screw the jars onto the lids and plant your moonbeams. And remember, because light charges glow-in-the-dark paint, you can give your moonbeams a boost by shining a flashlight on them to refresh their glow as needed.

Jar Band
Nightlight

Back in colonial times, tin punching was *de rigueur*. Punched panels not only added adornment to pie safe doors, but the tiny holes also provided air circulation. This was a serendipitous feature, as it helped prevent mold from growing and rotting the food stored within. Lanterns and candle carriers were made using punched tin as well. The piercings allowed for light to pass through while keeping the flame from blowing out and casting all into darkness. It's the last implementation of punched tin that serves as inspiration for this project: a jar band nightlight. Its punched pattern may look like a simple, decorative element, but in the middle of the night, it scares away the bogeyman.

Supplies

- 1 wide-mouth Mason jar band and lid • #000 extra fine steel wool • 1 inexpensive vertical night light with a plastic slide-on shade • Ruler • Tinsnips • White craft glue • Water • E6000 glue • Adhesive pearls, if desired • Aluminum wire • One 7-watt light bulb

MAKING YOUR NIGHT LIGHT

1. Buff the top of your Mason jar lid to a shine with the steel wool.

2. Remove the plastic shade from the nightlight. Measure the width of the indentation into which the shade used to slide, and, using tinsnips, cut a corresponding notch into the side of the band. Drill two small holes on each side of the back corners of the notch.

3. Use the lid as a template to gauge the writing area of your words—in this case, "to the Moon and Back." Write the saying on a piece of paper within the space allotted. Cut the circle from the paper, and glue it onto the top of the lid with white craft glue.

4. Using the hammer and nail, punch very small holes into the letters, following the font. The holes should be close, but not *too* close.

5. When the punching is finished, wet the paper and remove it from the lid. Glue the lid inside the band with the craft glue, making sure the notch is at the *bottom* of the saying.

6. Trim the outside of the jar band with adhesive pearls, if desired.

7. Thread two short lengths of wire through each of the holes you drilled into the band. Twist them securely to the band using a needle-nose pliers; then twist both free ends of the wire around the indentation in the night light into which the original shade used to slide.

8. Screw the 7-watt bulb into your new nightlight.

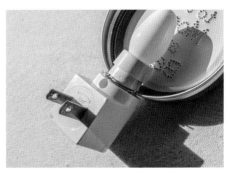

Moroccan Lantern
Trio

Mason jar fans everywhere know what the color "Ball blue" looks like. You can find examples of it in just about every antique shop in the United States. Colors like amethyst and peridot, on the other hand, are much more rare. And if you do find one for sale, its price might make you squirm. Luckily, there are less-expensive alternatives out there for lovers of colorful jars, for in 2013, Ball released the first in its Heritage Collection, which was a lovely blue pint jar. Spring green and purple followed the next two years. Other glass manufacturers jumped on board and started producing jars in varying colors. These, along with the Ball Heritage jars, can be found in craft stores and even big box stores.

Supplies

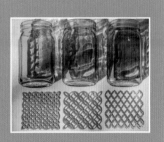

- Paper lace—metallic if you can find it, but you can also spray-paint white paper lace with metallic spray paint, as was done in this project • E6000 spray adhesive
- Quart-size, wide-mouth jars, the more colorful the better
- 14-gauge gold wire • Wire cutters • Needle-nose pliers
- Battery-operated candles

MAKING YOUR LANTERN TRIO

1. Spray-paint the paper lace, if necessary.

2. Spray E6000 to the back side of the lace and center it on the jars. (I applied lace to both the front and back of the jars in this project.)

3. With the wire cutter, cut two lengths of wire (one at 14" and another at 16") for each lantern you're making. With your hands, bend both wires into *U* shapes the approximate size of the jar's neck. With the needle-nose pliers, bend both ends of the 16" wire to form eyelets approximately ⅜" around.

4. Thread an eyelet onto each end of the shorter U-shaped wire, and slip the entire assembly onto the jar's neck.

5. Twist the free ends of the U-shaped wire with the pliers until snug around the neck of the jar. Bend the twist down toward the bottom of the jar for safety reasons.

6. Finally, add a battery-operated candle to each lantern to set a Moroccan mood.

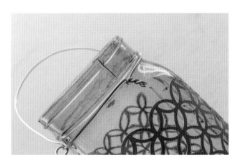

Ooh-La-La Fishnet Lanterns

I n his 1957 collection, *Mythologies*, French literary theorist Roland Barthes penned an essay entitled "Striptease." In it he enumerated the "classic props of the music hall." His list included, "the furs, the fans, the glove, the feathers, and the fishnet stocking." Much like apple pie and ice cream or peanut butter and jelly, feathers and fishnets have made, and will always make, a perfect pairing. Using them to turn a Mason jar into an alluring lantern takes minutes—if not seconds—leaving you time to concentrate on pairings of a different sort. Ooh-la-la.

Supplies

- 1 black fishnet anklet, approximately 9" long
- 1 quart-size, wide-mouth Mason jar
- 1 wide-mouth jar band
- 1 feather-embellished hair clip
- 1 battery-operated pillar candle

MAKING YOUR FISHNET LANTERNS

1. Start by slipping the anklet over the Mason jar from the bottom up.

2. Twist on the jar band over the anklet.

3. Fold the anklet over the band, gathering the excess around the jar's neck.

4. Attach the hair clip at a jaunty angle, and pop the battery-operated candle into the lantern.

Vintage Firefly
Lantern

Factoid #1: A typical incandescent light bulb is only 10-percent energy efficient, as the other 90 percent is lost as heat. A firefly's glow, on the other hand, is nearly 100-percent energy efficient. It has to be; otherwise the little bugger wouldn't survive its bioluminescent boogie.

Factoid #2: One of the not-so-magical ingredients that makes fireflies glow is called luciferin, from the Latin *lucifer*, which means "light-bringer." Although that might sound sinister, it's all science. To kids, fireflies are magical, which is why they're inclined to catching them in jars. It isn't the hardest thing to do, but it does force one into some damp situations, as fireflies like to hang out in the same places as mosquitos and the like. An easier, and less itchy, way to experience the enchantment of fireflies is to make a firefly lantern using tiny LED lights.

Supplies

- 1 small strand of 12 LED Moon Lights, powered by button batteries
- 1 vintage one-piece lid to fit the Mason jar used
- Foam tape
- 1 vintage Mason jar, any size will do

MAKING YOUR FIREFLY LANTERN

1. Attach the back of the button battery pack to the underside of the jar lid with a piece of foam tape.

2. Then, ease the LED light strand down into the jar and twist on the lid.

(*Bonus:* No fireflies were harmed in the making of this lantern.)

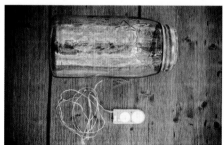

I n the early 1930s, Ernest Gantt of New Orleans, Louisiana, found himself in Los Angeles, California. He spotted an empty tailor's shop off Hollywood Boulevard and turned it into a small bar, which he named Don the Beachcomber. Mr. Gantt furnished it with a Polynesian flair, and, *voilà*, the tiki bar was born. It's said that Mr. Gantt also coined the term "tiki torch." The popularity of both his bar's theme and the torches with which he decorated it soon spread across the United States, delighting mai tai lovers everywhere.

Supplies

- 1 inexpensive metal tiki torch with a bamboo stake
- Utility scissors • Gloves • Hacksaw • Metal punch or drill and small bit • 1 regular-mouth jar lid and band
- 1 pint-size, regular-mouth Mason jar • Masking tape
- Jute twine • Craft glue, such as E6000
- Tinsnips or garden nipper • Tiki torch fuel

MAKING YOUR TIKI TORCH

1. Start by cutting the metal tiki container free from the bamboo prongs.

2. Unscrew the top—with the wick attached— off the tiki container. Use the hacksaw to cut off the threaded top of the container.

3. Punch or drill a starter hole in the center of the jar lid. With scissors, widen the hole in the lid to accept the container.

4. Thread the top of the tiki container through the hole in the jar lid. Screw the top with the wick back onto the container, feeding the wick through the hole in the jar lid.

5. Tuck the Mason jar into the bamboo stake's prongs. *Tightly* tape the top of the bamboo prongs together.

6. Lash the prongs together using the twine. Starting at the top of the jar, leave a 12" tail and loop the twine around the first prong, pulling taut as you go. Repeat looping back to the first prong, knot the twine, and reinforce with a dot of glue. Trim the ends of the twine.

7. Repeat the same process as above to loop the prongs together at the bottom of the jar.

8. Wrap twine around the bamboo pole—where the prongs just begin—and knot securely.

9. Remove the masking tape. Pop the lid into the jar band and screw the assembly onto the jar. Trim the bamboo prongs with a tin snips so they are just below the jar's band. Add tiki fuel to the jar.

Mercury Jar Lantern

ere's a little photographer's secret: dewdrops take close-up nature photography to new heights. Here's another secret: you can make your own faux drops with a simple spritz of water from a bottle. Or, if you want the dewdrops to be more pronounced and more stable, add some glycerine to the mix. This last trick is the perfect way to get a mercury glass effect on a jar, as I find using pure water too unpredictable. We're using the glycerine dewdrop technique in this project, but we're going to couple our glitzy mercury glass lantern with a rustic sisal rope handle for an interesting dichotomy.

Supplies

- A small spray bottle • Glycerine (found in the baking aisle of your grocery or craft store) • Water • 1 Mason jar— any size will do, but wide-mouth and squatty are best
- Mirror-finish spray paint • Paper towel • Sisal rope
- Glue gun and hot glue

MAKING YOUR MERCURY JAR LANTERN

1. Into the spray bottle, mix 1 to 2 teaspoons of glycerine with 4 ounces of water. Shake well.

2. Spray the glycerine mixture inside the jar, making sure to coat the glass as evenly as possible with droplets. (Don't worry if the mixture puddles on the bottom of the jar.)

3. While the glycerine drops are still wet, spray the inside of the jar with the mirror-finish spray paint, protecting the outside of the jar from overspray. When the paint is completely dry, invert the jar to drain any glycerine mixture and wipe the inside with a paper towel.

4. To make the lantern's handle, attach a length of sisal rope to each side of the jar's threaded neck with hot glue.

5. Wind and glue additional sisal rope around the neck to hide and secure the handle.

Washi Tape
Electric Up Light

Washi tape, also known as Japanese masking tape, burst onto the international crafting scene in 2006, and things haven't been the same since. Traditionally made of rice paper, the tape's beautiful colors, designs, and low tack make it a favorite among people of varying artistic talent everywhere. Another delightful aspect of washi tape is that it's translucent, which makes it perfect to embellish glass, or, in this case, a smooth Mason jar lampshade.

Supplies

- 1 smooth quart-size, regular-mouth Mason jar • Bottle cutter and finishing equipment
- One 4" square of scrap wood • Drill press or hand drill • Standard bits or Forstner bits that will accommodate the circumference of the socket, lamp cord, lamp nipple and nipple nut.
- 1 candelabra base socket cover • 1 keyless light bulb socket with a candelabra base
- 4" of standard threaded lamp nipple and nut to fit • Hacksaw • Sandpaper, if necessary
- White spray paint and primer • Lamp repair cord with integrated plug
- Washi tape, various colors • 15-watt candelabra light bulb or CFL equivalent

MAKING YOUR UP LIGHT

1. Cut approximately 1" off the bottom of the jar, and finish the cut edge according to the technical instructions in this book (p. 35–36).

2. Using a drill and the larger bit, drill a series of holes into one side of the 4" wood cube to create a circular hole slightly larger than the jar's mouth and deep enough to accept jar.

3. In the center of the hole, drill another hole big enough in circumference to accept the candelabra socket cover about 1½" deep.

4. In the center of that hole, drill a smaller hole to accept the lamp nipple. Drill through to the bottom of the block. At the bottom of the block, back-drill a hole slightly larger than the nipple nut.

5. Using the smaller bit, drill a hole to the side of the candelabra socket hole made in Step 3 for the cord. Drill until you reach the larger opening.

6. With a hacksaw, cut a length of lamp nipple to fit from the threaded bottom of the candelabra base to the bottom of the wooden block. Screw the lamp nipple into the candelabra base, and slip on the candelabra base cover.

7. Sand the cube and spray it with paint.

8. Thread the lamp cord through the hole in the side of the cube and up through the larger hole in the middle. Wire up the candelabra base's socket according to the manufacturer's directions. Feed the wired socket and nipple into the hole.

9. At the bottom of the wood block, thread on the lamp nipple's nut to secure the assembly.

10. To finish, apply lengths of colorful washi tape around the jar and screw in the light bulb.

Sparkling Outdoor Chandelier

dd twinkle lights to a backyard living space, and suddenly every warm summer evening is replete with romance and merriment. If that sounds like an oversell, it isn't. Take *al fresco* seating spaces at restaurants for example. Nearly all are decorated with twinkle lights. This outdoor chandelier, however, takes things a step further. First, it requires no electricity, and, second, even in the daytime when the lights aren't illuminated, the faceted gems playfully catch the sun. The chandelier can handle a light breeze, which only adds to its charm as it dances and "clinks" its way into your heart. That being said, please *do not* leave your chandelier out in inclement or windy weather.

Supplies

- 3 quart-size, regular-mouth Mason jars • Bottle cutter and finishing equipment
- One 8" tee duct cover (found in the heating and air conditioning department of big-box stores) • Drill • ⅛" drill bit and bit slightly larger than the chain's diameter, about ⅝" • 3 reproduction regular-mouth lids
- 10' of #16 single jack electro-galvanized chain • Needle-nose pliers
- Three ⅛" × ¾" fender washers • Three ¼" flat washers • Three #6-32 × ¾" zinc plated screws and nuts • 3 clear Bright Lights waterproof LED Bright Balls
- One 1" split ring • 6' of chained acrylic bead garland (found in the wedding aisle at craft stores)
- 3 large, faceted acrylic gem beads

MAKING YOUR CHANDELIER

1. Cut approximately 1" off the bottom of the jars and finish the cut edge according to the technical instructions in this book or according to the bottle cutter's instructions.

2. In the top of the tee cover, drill a ⅛" hole at its center and three ⅛" holes equally spaced around the perimeter, about 1½" from the outside edge. Then, on the side of the tee, drill three ⅛" holes approximately ⅛" up from the lower edge of the tee, making sure they are centered between each of the three holes previously drilled.

3. At the center of each jar lid, drill a ⅛" pilot hole and then follow up with a ⁵⁄₁₆" bit to widen the hole to accept the jack chain.

4. With needle-nose pliers, separate the chain into six lengths: four at 10", one at 18", and one at 24". Open the loops at both ends of the chains. Set three of the 10" lengths aside. Feed one opened link of the remaining 10" chain-end through a fender washer and then up through one of the three outside holes in the top of the tee cover. With the pliers, close the link at the top of the tee cover. Repeat with the last step using the 18" and 24" chain lengths.

(continued on next page)

MAKING YOUR CHANDELIER
(continued from p. 139)

5. At the bottom end of the chains just installed, thread on the reproduction jar lids, following up with the ¼" flat washers.

6. Thread one nut onto each of the #6-32 × ¾" screws.

7. Measure up 4" from the end of the chain and thread one #6-32 × ¾" screw and nut assembly into the link and secure with a second nut. (These screws and nuts will keep the individual jars in place and will allow you to move them upward along the chains to perform light maintenance.) Repeat this for the other two chains.

8. At the bottom of each chain, attach a light ball, and close the links with the needle-nose pliers. Feed the light ball through the top of each jar and screw on the lids. Each jar should be able to move side to side and back and forth freely without touching one of the other two jars!

9. Attach the remaining three 10" lengths of chain to the chain loops that protrude from the top of the tee. Crimp all the links closed with the pliers. Gather up these three lengths of the chain and slip their links into the split ring. Close the links with the pliers.

10. Open the beaded garland chain into lengths of approximately 9", 13", 17", and 29". Attach a large-faceted gem bead to one end of each garland chain.

11. Attach the longest length of chain to the center of the tee cover using a leftover link from the jack chain. Straighten one side of the link and feed it through the center hole of the tee cover. Using the needle-nose pliers, twist the link closed, and attach the longest length of garland to the link protruding from the underside of the tee cover.

12. Attach the remaining three lengths of garland into the small holes in the side of the tee cover.

CONVERSIONS

Metric Equivalent

Inches (in.)	Feet (ft.)	Yards (yd.)	Millimeters (mm)	Centimeters (cm)	Meters (m)
1/64			0.40		
1/32			0.79		
1/25			1		
1/16			1.59		
1/8			3.18		
1/4			6.35		
3/8			9.53	0.95	
2/5			10	1	
1/2			12.7	1.27	
5/8			15.9	1.59	
3/4			19.1	1.91	
7/8			22.2	2.22	
1			25.4	2.54	
2			50.8	5.08	
3			76.2	7.62	
4			101.6	10.16	
5			127	12.7	
6			152	15.2	
7			178	17.8	
8			203	20.3	
9			229	22.9	
10			254	25.4	
11			279	27.9	
12	1		305	30.5	.30
36	3	1	914	91.4	.91
39.4	3 1/12	1 1/12	1,000	100	1.00

Converting Temperatures

Convert degrees Fahrenheit (F) to degrees Celsius (C) by following this simple formula: Subtract 32 from the Fahrenheit temperature reading. Then mulitply that number by 5/9.

For example, 77°F - 32 = 45. 45 × 5/9 = 25°C.

To convert degrees Celsius to degrees Fahrenheit, multiply the Celsius temperature reading by 9/5, then add 32.

For example, 25°C × 9/5 = 45. 45 + 32 = 77°F.

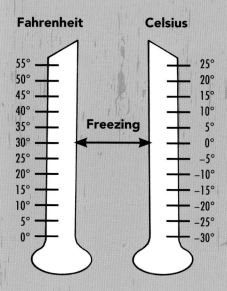

Converting Measurements

TO CONVERT:	TO:	MULTIPLY BY:	TO CONVERT:	TO:	MULTIPLY BY:
Inches	Millimeters	25.4	Millimeters	Inches	0.039
Inches	Centimeters	2.54	Centimeters	Inches	0.394
Feet	Meters	0.305	Meters	Feet	3.28
Yards	Meters	0.914	Meters	Yards	1.09
Miles	Kilometers	1.609	Kilometers	Miles	0.621
Square inches	Square centimeters	6.45	Square centimeters	Square inches	0.155
Square feet	Square meters	0.093	Square meters	Square feet	10.8
Square yards	Square meters	0.836	Square meters	Square yards	1.2
Cubic inches	Cubic centimeters	16.4	Cubic centimeters	Cubic inches	0.061
Cubic feet	Cubic meters	0.0283	Cubic meters	Cubic feet	35.3
Cubic yards	Cubic meters	0.765	Cubic meters	Cubic yards	1.31
Pints (US)	Liters	0.473 (Imp. 0.568)	Liters	Pints (US)	2.114 (Imp. 1.76)
Quarts (US)	Liters	0.946 (Imp. 1.136)	Liters	Quarts (US)	1.057 (Imp. 0.88)
Gallons (US)	Liters	3.785 (Imp. 4.546)	Liters	Gallons (US)	0.264 (Imp. 0.22)
Ounces	Grams	28.4	Grams	Ounces	0.035
Pounds	Kilograms	0.454	Kilograms	Pounds	2.2
Tons	Metric tons	0.907	Metric tons	Tons	1.1

RESORCES

Publications

The Art of Preserving All Kinds of Animal and Vegetable Substances for Several Years by Nicolas Appert

US Department of Agriculture Farmers' Bulletin 359, *Canning Vegetables in the Home* by J.F. Breazeale

The Fruit Jar Works (volumes 1 and 2) by Alice Creswick

The Red Book by Douglas M. Leybourne

The Illustrated Guide to Collecting Bottles by Cecil Munsey

From Great Aunt May's Cellar by Arleta Rodrigues and Alice Creswick

The Standard Fruit Jar Reference by Dick Roller

Encyclopedia of Kitchen History by Mary Ellen Snodgrass

Fruit Jars: A Collectors' Manual by Julian Harrison Toulouse

Articles

"A Primer on Fruit Jars," by Dave Hinson, www.av.qnet.com/~glassman/info/b&e/primer.htm

"Frequently Asked Questions—Fruit Jars," by Dave Hinson, www.av.qnet.com/~glassman/info/jarfaq.htm

"Canning Tomatoes, Growing 'Better and More Perfect Woman' The Girls' Tomato Club Movement," by Elizabeth Engelhardt, www.durhamcountylibrary.org/exhibits/jeanes/canning_tomatoes_growing.pdf

Websites

Midwest Antique Fruit Jar & Bottle Club, www.fruitjar.org

Collectors Weekly, www.collectorsweekly.com (search "fruit jars")

The Federation of Historical Bottle Collectors, www.fohbc.org

For Ball-specific history, visit Minnetrista, www.minnetrista.net

"A Legacy Etched in Glass," www.vimeo.com/96710414

The Society of Historical Archaeology's Historic Glass Bottle Identification & Information Website www.sha.org/bottle

SUPPLIES

Although many supplies were used to make the projects included in *Mason Jar Nation*, several items deserve a special shout-out for both quality and indispensability:

Creator's Premium Bottle Cutter (pictured on page 35)

Ephrem's Bottle Cutter (also pictured on page 35)

Ironton Heavy-Duty Hole Puncher (pictured on page 33)

E6000 glue, both the spray and tube-variety

Armor Etch Glass Etching Cream

Rust-Oleum Mirror Effect spray paint

ABOUT THE AUTHOR

JoAnn Moser is a writer, DIYer, and photographer. She has been a contributing writer to Curbly.com, an online design community, since 2006. Her original projects can be found there as well as at DIYmaven.com. With an MFA in creative writing from Hamline University, she also spins stories of the fictional variety, several of which have been featured in *Alfred Hitchcock Mystery Magazine*. When she's not writing, DIYing, or taking pictures, she's reading, walking, camping, or binge-watching something on Netflix. She lives in Minnesota with her partner in life and in DIY, Nick.